MAKING TRADITIONAL AND MODERN
Chutneys, Pickles and Relishes
A COMPREHENSIVE GUIDE

J. C. Jeremy Hobson and Philip Watts

THE CROWOOD PRESS

First published in 2010 by
The Crowood Press Ltd
Ramsbury, Marlborough
Wiltshire SN8 2HR

www.crowood.com

Photography Acknowledgements

Unless otherwise indicated, the photographs in this book were taken by
Philip Watts and are his copyright. The authors and publishers are grateful to
Rupert Stephenson for providing one additional photograph.

British Library Cataloguing-in-Publication Data

A catalogue record for this book is available from the British Library.

ISBN 978 1 84797 192 0

Originated by The Manila Typesetting Company

Printed and bound in Singapore by Craft Print International Ltd

Contents

Acknowledgements   4

An Introduction and the Overseas Influence   6

1   Utensils, Hygiene and Storage   12

2   Choosing the Right Ingredients   25

3   Recipes for Characterful Chutneys   40

4   Recipes for Pickles and Pickling   74

5   Recipes for Relishes, Ketchups, Marinades and Dips   99

6   How to Use Chutneys and Pickles   126

Glossary   135

At a Glance Recipe List   139

Index   142

Acknowledgements

As always, there are several people to thank in connection with the compilation of this book, not least of whom are Lawrence and Julia Murphy, *Fat Olives*, Emsworth, Hampshire; Chris and Sarah Whitehead, Whites@the Clockhouse, Tenbury Wells, Worcestershire; and Jonathan Waters, also at Whites@the Clockhouse, Tenbury Wells, Worcestershire. Special thanks too must go to Lynn Brodie and Mary Hart – the latter of whom was kind enough to let us riffle through her considerable recipe stocks and include many of them within the pages of this book.

Others who have helped tremendously in supplying recipes and in all sorts of other ways are (and in no particular order) Beryl Woodhouse; Mariangela Karlovitch, the Medusa Resort Hotel, Naxos, Greece; Valerie Hardy; Samantha Coley; Ann Lambert; Ann Brockhurst; Kathy Neuteboom of Stonham Hedgerow Ltd, Ipswich, Suffolk (www.stonhamhedgerow.co.uk); Chris and Felicity Stockwell; Sally Hallstead; the Country Women's Institute of Australia; Alexios Theophilus; Theo Cartwright; Andy Hook at *Blackfriars Restaurant*, Newcastle; Robin Harford of www.EatWeeds.co.uk; Hall & Woodhouse, family brewers, Blandford St Mary, Dorset; Edd McArdle; Simon Adams and Rosie Robinson who were, at the time of writing, at *The Stephan Langton*, Friday Street, near Dorking, Surrey; Michael Stamford; Andrew and Jacquie Pern at the *Star Inn*, Harome, Helmsley, North Yorkshire; Stella Boldy and Doreen Allars.

We have particular cause to be grateful to Tom Stobart's book, *The Cook's Encyclopaedia: Ingredients and Processes*, published by B.T. Batsford in 1980 – without it and its particular definitions we would have not found compiling our book quite so easy. Thank you to Lucy Smith of Anova Books for granting permission to quote from its pages. Thanks, too, to Louise Bilham of the rights department of ITV plc for using all her efforts to gain permission to include the recipes that first appeared in *Farmhouse Kitchen II*, published in 1978 by Trident International Television Enterprises Ltd.

AUTHORS' NOTE

It has obviously been impossible to test every recipe included within these pages. All have, however, been offered in good faith by well-respected chefs: the winners of various trophies at relevant events large and small, amateur cooks, enthusiastic family members and friends, all of whom assure us that their recipes work. Sometimes, however, they have been a little lax in their quantities or methods and, rather than imposing upon them again for yet another favour, we have used our discretion in order to make logical assumptions regarding weights, alternative ingredients or cooking times. The making of country chutneys, pickles and relishes is not, after all, an exact science – a point which the newcomer to this method of preserving should always bear in mind.

Also, whilst not doubting in any way their veracity, we cannot guarantee that any recipes given by anyone have not been adapted from those that have already previously appeared in books or on the Internet (bearing in mind the fact that many 'classic' recipes have, over a period of time, come into the public domain). Therefore, should anyone reading this book feel that their own recipes have been taken without permission, we can only offer our apologies and the promise that, if they contact us via the publishers, we will make suitable amends in any future reprints.

WEIGHTS AND MEASURES

Some of the older recipes included in this book have been converted to metric from imperial; a practice that cannot be carried out precisely. For instance, 1oz is actually equal to 28.35 grams, so it is not really possible to measure accurately 25 or 30 grams if you are using imperial measuring spoons, jugs and scales. The same applies to liquid measurements, so, in order to avoid complications, we have in some instances rounded the conversions up or down.

AND FINALLY ...

The mention of any products, or manufacturers of products, in the text does not in any way mean that they have our endorsement!

J. C. Jeremy Hobson
Philip Watts
Summer 2010

A row of chutneys and pickles makes you look forward to the next occasion they can be used!

An Introduction and the Overseas Influence

Living in the rural countryside, 'Granny' did, quite often, know best when it came to preserving summer and autumn produce in order that it could be safely eaten all year round. Worldwide, chutneys, pickles and relishes were created, not only to use up surplus fruit and vegetables, but also to mask the taste of meat and fish that may have been past its best, or to spice up what might otherwise have proved to be a bland and boring meal. In all its various forms and for whatever reason, creative chutneys and pickle-making was a practice that began many, many generations ago – although it proved to be particularly important in some of the more austere years of the twentieth century, when food was hard to come by and what was available needed the addition of something to make it more interesting. (Yes, even the eating of wartime luncheon meat was apparently made almost pleasurable by the inclusion of a spoonful or two of chutney – which did, however, have the effect of making chutney less popular after World War II because it brought back memories of hard times.)

During the final, wealthy decades of the twentieth century, however, the Western world possessed more money than possibly ever before and it became, on the whole (with the exception of a few diehards), pretty much a 'throwaway society', with the result that it was almost unthinkable that anyone would bother making their own chutneys, pickles and relishes, when there were some perfectly acceptable and certainly more easily obtained examples to be found on the supermarket shelves. However, since then, various financial crises, the need to cut down on air miles, an increasing interest in smallholding and a desire to get 'back to nature' – together with the popularity of attractive produce being seen by those who would like to use it properly and frugally – have brought some of both Granny's principles and Far Eastern cooking techniques back into vogue.

Modern-thinking cooks with a view to the countryside and the sourcing of local produce have not missed any opportunity to utilize traditional recipes and, in some circumstances, have even given them a modern and exciting twist. Recent interest in the art and skills associated with making pickles and chutneys has ensured that the relevant classes in the 'produce' sections of village and county shows no longer merely contain a few pots produced by the older generation of stalwarts, but are now also enthusiastically supported by much younger contestants of both sexes. Farm shops report that, when customers come in to stock up on fresh vegetables, they almost always peruse the shelves containing attractively packaged pickles, chutneys and relishes and, having done so, invariably take one or two jars away with them.

Has anyone failed to be pleased with a small Christmas hamper of pickles and chutneys? We don't think so – okay, they might not have quite the same cachet as a De Beers diamond or the keys to a Ferrari, but they will, nevertheless, be brought out and enjoyed during the following few weeks and months. Home-produced pickles and chutneys will therefore make perfect small gifts, especially if presented in unusually shaped or pretty containers that are pleasingly labelled – not a difficult job in these days of computer-design programs.

As well as being given as gifts, pickles and chutneys make useful additions to any charity fund-raising event and will, like the ones on display in the farm shop or at the farmers' market, soon disappear from the table top from which they are being sold. So, selling pickles and chutneys is no longer the preserve (forgive the pun) of the Women's Institute or regional branches of the Townswomen's Guild. There are, however, as with so many things appertaining to modern living, certain legalities to which one must adhere when making and selling produce for public purchase and consumption. It will therefore pay to check whether, in order to do so, you need to have your 'production premises' inspected by environmental health officers and any weights and measures approved by trading standards. Remember that all local councils are different. Making chutneys and pickles to sell for profit requires much the same approach (and may also require you to

Home-produced chutneys and pickles look even better when they are attractively labelled and pleasingly packaged.

There are certain legalities to which one must adhere when making and selling produce for public purchase and consumption – even at the most local of affairs.

be registered with the local council), but could be well worthwhile in the long run. While farmers' markets were originally set up to provide local farmers with a direct outlet to the public, the National Farmers' Retail & Markets Association (FARMA) is also keen to encourage what it jargonistically terms 'non-farming secondary food producers'.

THE OVERSEAS INFLUENCE

Defining pickles is reasonably straightforward, which is more than can be said for identifying the exact differences between what is a chutney or a relish, where there can be an element of crossover – as will be seen later in this section and also in the main chapter dealing with recipes. Basically, pickling is simply a method of preserving food by immersing it in brine or vinegar. There is some evidence that the word pickle is derived from the Germanic word *pekel*, meaning 'brine', but it is also known that the word was in existence in the English language of medieval times when it was variously spelled as *pekille, pykyl, pekkyll,* or *pykulle.* Although it would not have been known as such, the actual method of pickling has been used since at least Roman times as a means of preserving fruit and vegetables during times of a glut. Cleopatra, Pliny, Julius Caesar and Tiberius were, according to the writings of the Ancients, all avid consumers of pickles (in far more recent times, Napoleon insisted that his catering corps carried portable, preserved fruits and vegetables with which to feed his invading armies).

Despite now being associated with traditional and regional UK foods, especially cold meats and, latterly, the ubiquitous pub 'Ploughman's Lunch' (which is, incidentally, a creation of some 1960s adman's imagination rather than, as is often supposed, a centuries-old farmer's hunger-beating standby), chutneys actually originated in India and were first mentioned in British cooking books in the 1600s. The name is a derivation of the word *chatni*, which was used to describe a strong, sweet relish, but in particularly old books it is often written as *chutnee*. Its appearance in Britain and elsewhere came about as a result of the development of trade with India; ideas and cooking methods had been brought home, but the ingredients altered in order to make use of whatever produce was available locally (a sentiment that should apply equally to today's chutney makers). Experts agree that there is a huge difference between what is known as chutney in India and surrounding countries (normally a mixed paste of raw, freshly harvested and ground ingredients) and the much sweeter tasting (cooked and preserved) chutneys found in the Western hemisphere. Somewhat confusingly, any Indian traditionalist tasting such a chutney would probably describe it as a sweet pickle!

And the confusion doesn't stop there, as what we call a chutney in the UK might be referred to by an American as a relish! When the various people involved with this book were questioned as to what they considered to be the essential difference between a chutney and a relish, most of them simply described a relish as being thin chutney — which is no real help at all! Further research, however, indicates that relishes are made in

The Ploughman's Lunch is a creation of some 1960s adman's imagination rather than, as is often supposed, a centuries-old tradition.

different ways throughout the world and many are, in fact, a cross between a pickle and chutney. Others are thickened by flour and made creamy by the inclusion of local yogurt. Perhaps the easiest definition to give is that relishes were, in their original form, accompaniments to a main meal, or were a type of cooking marinade, and were often made at the last minute using whatever ingredients were available. Being fabricated from freshly gathered produce and having little or no preserving ingredients included, they obviously had limited 'shelf life'. Relishes are perhaps best known in America, where they undoubtedly originated as a result of Mexican and Spanish immigrants bringing with them traditional salsa recipes. Incidentally, even accepting that the word *salsa* is basically a Spanish word for sauce, it is impossible to understand why the same word should be used to describe a kind of dance music of Cuban origin – perhaps it's because the elements of jazz and rock music encourage a 'saucy' dance from the participants?

Think of America and one cannot help but imagine commercially produced tomato ketchup being spread in great, unnaturally coloured globules of gunk on top of a burger, but it is only in the West where the name has become synonymous with such eating habits. In Javanese cooking, for example, ketjap is a type of soy sauce, which quite often includes a salty fish base and either molasses or brown sugar. Other sources have it that the word *ketchup* is derived from the Chinese language. According to Tom Stobart writing in *The Cook's Encyclopaedia*, the cookery books of the nineteenth century abounded with ketchup recipes – oyster ketchup (oysters with white wine, brandy, sherry, shallots and spices), mussel ketchup (mussels and cider), pontac or pontack ketchup (elderberries), Windermere ketchup (mushrooms and horseradish), wolfram ketchup (beer, anchovies and mushrooms) and others based on walnuts, cucumber or indeed, almost any other ingredient that happened to capture the cook's imagination.

ALL ROUTES LEAD TO HOME

No matter from where they might originate, pickles, chutneys and relishes are known worldwide – so much so that in Australia the word 'chutney' was used as a metaphor in 'Chutney Generations', the world's first ever exhibition tracing the extremely complex Fiji-Indian identity, which was staged at the Liverpool Regional Museum in Sydney from December 2006 to February 2007. In the context of the exhibition, it compared the fusion, culture, dreams, ideals, ideologies and history of Fijian-Indian migrants across the globe as being similar to the process of making chutney, that is, where ingredients are blended to the point where there is no single identity (an arguable notion when one considers that all of those we have met in connection with this book insist that every single one of the ingredients of chutneys should complement one another). Not content with such a simile, the organizers of the exhibition went on to coin a new word, describing the coalition of the Australian-Fiji-Indian community as being a 'chutnification'!

At the other end of the world, there is, of course, the traditional pickled herring to be found in Norway. Less well known is the fact that Norwegians have a recipe for poached cod – which is apparently best served with a green tomato pickle. In-between, the African continent has a whole plethora of mainly vegetable-based relishes, many of which started life in the seemingly inhospitable Sahara, and also includes the Tanzanian speciality

Norwegian pickled herrings.

of horseradish relish, traditionally served with boiled beef – not too far different from England's long-established Sunday roast.

We might be pushing the connection, but there's also the question of coleslaw being a type of relish. The basic description is that it is simply a salad consisting mainly of shredded raw cabbage, but there are several variations, many of which include typical chutney, pickle, relish and dip ingredients and need the addition of oil and vinegar to make them work.

Reading *Making Traditional and Modern Chutneys, Pickles and Relishes* will, we hope, turn you from being perhaps merely an interested bystander into an enthusiastic and dedicated participant of an age-old science, which has, once again, come to the forefront of modern cooking. If you enjoy the country life and can participate in it by growing some of your own produce, all well and good. If you live in the town and source your ingredients via the High Street greengrocer or through weekend trips to market towns, pick-your-owns or even from the hedgerow, you will not be disappointed by the recipes included here. Wherever you live and no matter how they are produced, we guarantee that, every time you open your cupboards and see a batch of jars or bottles catching the light and glowing full of autumnal colour, you will smile and look forward to the next occasion they can be used.

Utensils, Hygiene and Storage

Making chutneys, pickles and relishes is not, to use today's jargon, 'rocket science'. It is a cost-effective thing to do, requiring very little in the way of specialized equipment and ingredients, which, when chosen for their seasonal availability, should be cheap enough, or even free. Nevertheless, there are some basic cooking and preparation utensils required and also, for obvious health reasons, a certain understanding of the need for hygiene in preparation, bottling and storage. But it is all extremely therapeutic, even ritualistic: old jam jars and pickle pots are retrieved from where they've previously been stored, washed in the sink, then sterilized in the oven; preserving pans are removed from the top of the kitchen cupboard (and the resident spider made homeless); funnels and wooden spatulas are recovered from whatever job the children have been using them for; and, finally, a decision has to be made as to what recipe best suits the surplus produce currently on offer. Oh, and then there's time, of course; it can be a long process, so it's as well to be sure that you have everything to hand before you start.

UTENSILS

Although some of the equipment necessary is quite specialized (a decent preserving pan, for instance), much of what you need, such as wooden spoons, will already be part of the contents of the average kitchen drawer. Anything that does need to be bought will, however, be relatively easy to source. Look in the right shop dealing specifically with such items and you should be able to find all the tools, utensils and storage equipment necessary to pickle produce and make chutneys at any time of the year. In other retail outlets, they seem to be a seasonal addition to the shelves and appear just in time to coincide with the 'season of mists and mellow fruitfulness', as described by John Keats in his poem of 1819, *Ode to Autumn*. Some of the best places to look for specific equipment are your local garden centre or country store. If you happen to be visiting France, or, in fact, any European country where the art of preserving surplus fruit and vegetables is a regular part of rural life, the hypermarket there will also prove to be very useful. Of the specialist outlets in the UK, it appears, from talking to several people in connection with this book, that Lakeland Ltd is a firm favourite. Lakeland prides itself on being 'the home of creative kitchenware' and, judging from the content of its High Street shops and online 'virtual catalogue', we see no reason to disbelieve the claim.

It is best to have all of your likely equipment and ingredients to hand before making a start.

Pots and Pans

Not many households will have a large enough cooking pot for making vast quantities of chutney, therefore the acquisition of a suitable vessel will be essential. It will also undoubtedly be your largest financial outlay, so you might as well buy the best to start with. If it is manufactured and sold expressly for the job, there will be no concerns regarding the material from which it is made, but otherwise it is best to ensure that it is stainless steel or aluminium – there are devotees of both. Other materials – iron, copper or brass, for example – could cause whatever it is you are preserving to become tainted. Enamelled pans are recommended by a few, but dismissed by many, because of the fact that they will eventually become chipped and therefore difficult to keep clean and sterilized.

Whilst big heavy-bottomed saucepans can be used, one of the problems of doing so is that because they are generally straight-sided, air flow is restricted, cooking takes longer and there is more chance of the pan's contents becoming burnt. Preserving pans are typically wider at the top than the bottom and, depending from what material they have been made, might be 'double-layered' or 'encapsulated'. Stainless steel, for example, is known to be a poor conductor of heat, so an encapsulated base (where a disc of aluminium has been sandwiched between two stainless-steel discs on the bottom) will make heat conduction that much more effective. Stainless steel is also attractive to look at (and, due to its size, your pan might need to be on permanent display rather than tucked away in a kitchen cupboard), easy to clean and maintain, robust and long-lasting. Choose a pan that is easy to use; some have bucket-type handles, with further aid being given by the addition of a smaller 'helper' handle attached to one edge.

A decent-sized preserving pan is essential.

There is generally never any need for a pan to have a lid, as the contents of preserving pans are usually cooked with the lid off. Leaving a lid on chutney whilst cooking will simply cause condensation and resultant water, whereas the idea should be to allow liquid to evaporate slowly during the heating process.

With relishes and the like, the quantities and volumes will be much smaller, so almost any good quality heavy-bottomed pan that fits the above criteria will suffice. There is also the obvious difference between the cooking times of chutneys and relishes, the latter being cooked for very short periods, so a robust pan is not quite so necessary for relishes.

Spoons and Ladles

Mary Hart, of Morden, Surrey, is a winner of innumerable prizes for her chutneys and preserves. She recommends that you always keep special spoons and spatulas for chutneys. Ideally, they should be large enough to handle easily and should always be made of wood – beech wood, for preference. She also offers a little tip, in that it can be useful to mark the handle of your favourite spoon in such a way that when it is standing vertically in the bottom of a pan, the various marks will indicate certain liquid volumes – which will save having to continually remeasure them on future occasions. A decent wooden spoon should also have a strong handle, because quantities of chutney ingredients can be quite heavy as they begin to thicken and come together. A less well created handle might not stand the rigour of continual stirring – especially when coming towards the end of cooking time when it is vital to keep stirring in order to prevent the contents from sticking to the base of the pan and burning.

Ladles should be chosen with thought for their use. A 100g/3½oz ladle is quite a handy one to have, as it is not too big and cumbersome to enable careful bottle and jar filling without spilling most of its contents over the work surface!

Funnels and Sieves

A wide-mouthed funnel will be essential for bottling up chutneys and pickles, but its neck (the piece that goes into the jar or bottle) should not be as long or as tapered as the usual household type, otherwise it will prove impossible to 'feed' what are often quite chunky finished products through the narrow aperture.

Whilst you probably won't need to sieve many, if any, of the chutneys and pickles found in this book, you will nevertheless need to use a fine, preferably nylon, sieve for some of the ketchups and relishes. A sieve might also be useful for straining spiced vinegar.

Jars and Bottles

It seems that provided they are clean and sterilized, it matters little what shape or type of jar or bottle are used. They should, of course, be wide-necked enough to allow the filling of them to be carried out without too much mishap and mess. There is, however, something to be said for them being more or less uniform in size, as you will then quickly learn just how much quantity of chutney, pickle or relish will fill a certain number. All being the same size, they are also rather easier to store. Odd, smaller jars do,

Funnels of varying sizes will prove invaluable when it comes to bottling and storing.

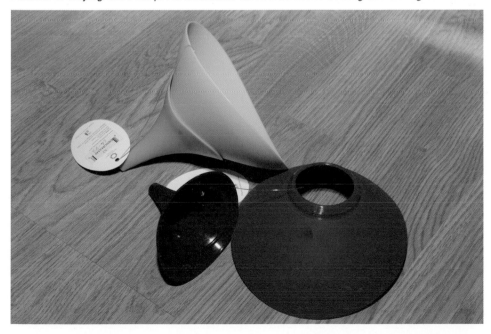

nevertheless, have their place; when, for instance, you wish to make up a selection to give away as presents, or for those occasions when a small quantity of chutney remains in the pan, yet is too much to throw away.

Although more expensive to purchase initially (other jars often being obtained via recycling methods), Kilner, Le Parfait and similar jar types are undoubtedly the best. With the original Kilner jars, a glass disc sat on top of the jar and was then secured in place with a metal screw band which contained a rubber seal. Nowadays, both sections are usually made from metal, so great care needs to be exercised in order to ensure that vinegar cannot come into contact with and 'eat' through the metal parts.

The original Kilner jar is sometimes confused with the type of preserving jar that is glass-lidded, rubber-sealed and kept tightly closed by the addition of a very clever, yet simple to operate, wired catch. The latter are arguably your best option and certainly well worth considering. They can be used in the conventional way for storing, or, if making large quantities of produce, it might be an idea to store it initially in big jars for six months or so and then, whenever is convenient and you have more time, spoon the contents into smaller, more acceptable-sized receptacles. Many garden centres sell mini glass-lidded jars that will prove perfect when it is intended to give some of your produce to friends and relatives as presents.

Friends and family will no doubt help in keeping and collecting their empty jars on your behalf – especially if there is the promise of the odd jar full of this year's produce

The original Kilner jar is sometimes confused with the type of preserving jar that is glass-lidded, rubber-sealed and kept tightly closed by the addition of a very clever, yet simple to operate, wired catch.

Many garden centres sell mini glass-lidded jars that are perfect to give away as presents.

in appreciative thanks for their efforts. There are also some garden centres and 'pick-your-own' places that act as a collecting point for clean glass jars and sauce bottles, from where you can pick up any amount in return for a donation placed in the collecting tin of the owner's favourite charity. Some commercial manufacturers sell their beers and lemonades in bottles that have a porcelain-type stopper which is sealed by a rubber ring and a wire device. These are undoubtedly one of the best recycling alternatives when considering making and storing ketchups and similar sauces.

Make sure that all recycled glass is clean and untainted by the smell of its last resident, such as curry, coffee, tomato sauce and the like. To make absolutely sure, one little tip is to sprinkle into it a good tablespoon of bicarbonate of soda and add a 'splosh' of boiling water (a 'splosh' being more than the 'glug' so often spoken of by TV chefs!). Rub the solution over all the surfaces and leave for a couple of minutes before rinsing out well in cold water.

One last tip about glass jars: if you warm them before placing hot produce in them, you will reduce the risk of the glass cracking.

Lids and Covers
All agree that whilst it is okay continually to reuse jars and bottles, you should never do the same with the lids. Lids need to fit tightly in order to create a vacuum and they will not necessarily do so if reused several times over. For this reason, it might be a good idea after all to use a single uniform size of jar in order that new lids of the relevant

dimension may be more easily purchased – normally they can be bought in packs of 100 for about £8 to £9. Metal lids should have a plastic-type coating to prevent the pickling vinegar eating into them. If, for some reason, you do end up using unprotected metal lids, be sure to include discs of ceresin paper (obtainable from most chemists). Whilst on the subject of lids and covers of one type or another, although these are normally more applicable to jam making than they are to chutneys and pickles, it is nevertheless worth mentioning that it is possible to buy kits containing wax seals, cellophane covers, elastic bands and labels from shops such as Lakeland Ltd and these may prove useful to have on occasions as 'emergency backup'.

If using jars with a Kilner-type two-piece lid, once filled with chutney they should seal themselves during cooling, as the lid gets sucked down by the vacuum created because of the contents contracting inside the jar. To test that a jar is sealed correctly, gently remove the screw band and tap the lid with the base of a teaspoon – a clear ringing sound indicates a good seal, whereas a dull 'thud' suggests that it has not sealed effectively. Alternatively, press the middle of the lid with your index finger: if the lid springs up once your finger has been removed, there is no seal. Either test should only be conducted after the jars and their contents have cooled for between twelve to twenty-four hours.

To add to the attractiveness of a presentation gift of chutney or pickles, cover the lid with a small circle of pretty material, or perhaps a piece of old-fashioned brown wrapping paper tied securely round the bottle neck with a piece of raffia. For extra safety and to add to the overall appearance of ketchups being given as gifts, their corks may be further sealed with a blob of candle wax and stamped with the family crest!

More Essentials

Kitchen scales are a must, as are measuring jugs and a couple of large Pyrex-type glass mixing bowls. As well as glass, the old-fashioned earthenware-type of mixing bowl will also suffice – provided that it is not crazed or cracked. A bowl is essential for some of the pickle recipes where things need to be tossed and coated with ground spice, and also for the times when it may be necessary to leave ingredients to stand overnight after being sprinkled with salt to extract unwanted moisture. Good quality stainless-steel knives should be the mainstay of any kitchen, but it might pay to make sure that there is as least one with a thick-enough blade and a safe handle to ensure that when slicing through cabbage and other solid vegetables, it can be done with the least amount of personal risk. Kitchen roll will prove invaluable throughout all the various stages of creating chutneys, pickles and relishes. Labels are definite essentials if you are ever to have any hope of keeping track of what each jar and bottle contains and when it was made.

Some non-essential yet useful extra items of equipment might include: wooden boards on which to stand your jars and bottles whilst in the process of filling them; pestle and mortars or a small coffee grinder (to break down whole spices); muslin to make bundles of *bouquet garni*; and several tea towels to gain an extra grip on things and to protect your hands on occasion. Ordinary cardboard boxes are a good way of storing jars of chutneys and pickles, because of the simple fact that square boxes are easier to place for safe keeping than irregular-sized and round jars. They also keep the contents clean and out of unnecessary light.

It is possible to buy jars, lids and all manner of equipment from retail outlets such as Lakeland Ltd – and the boxes they come in are useful for storing the finished produce.

HYGIENE

General kitchen hygiene is basically the same no matter what you are cooking. Kitchens have the potential to be a breeding ground for all kinds of nasty moulds and bacteria, so keeping your surface areas and kitchen cabinets clean will go a long way to ensuring a hygienic food preparation area. Surfaces should be cleaned daily and certainly before you are about to start preparing to make chutneys, pickles and relishes. Match your cleaning product to your surface type, but steer clear of any abrasives because they will shorten the lifespan of the surfaces – in fact, you could consider using items that you will already have as cooking ingredients as cleaning substances. Baking soda, for instance, is suitable for removing most common household stains from surfaces. Use two or three table-spoons of baking soda per cup of warm water and gently remove grease and stubborn splatters with a sponge. Afterwards, rinse down with cold water and dab with a paper towel. Alternatively, use a combination of equal parts vinegar and warm water.

A few tips regarding kitchen hygiene when making chutneys and the like include: wiping up liquid spills immediately they occur; not using newspapers on which to stand your jars and bottles as you fill them – the ink can seep into the surface finishing and leave stubborn marks; and, instead of sliding objects across surfaces, pick them up, thereby minimizing the risk of scratching and creating a potential breeding ground for bacteria.

All equipment must be spotless before beginning making chutneys, pickles and relishes.

Making chutney can be a messy business, so for ease, as well as health reasons, keep all surfaces as clean as possible.

Cloths and Sponges

Making chutneys and relishes can be a messy affair and it will not be long before some are spilt. The natural reaction is obviously to wipe them up straight away, but if you do so with less than clean cloths and sponges, there is always the danger that you will be contaminating rather than cleaning. Recent research by the Royal London Hospital noted that many domestic kitchen cloths and sponges tested were harbouring bacteria that could be responsible for *E. coli* and *Salmonella* infections.

Keep your cloths and sponges clean by washing them in hot, soapy water, then placing them in a suitable disinfectant before rinsing and allowing them to dry thoroughly. There is, apparently, nothing to be gained in soaking them overnight – disinfectant solutions weaken over a period of time. Alternatively, heat them for one minute in a microwave, or place them in a dishwasher operating with a drying cycle. Sponges that were put through either a dishwasher or a microwave were found to hold less than 1 per cent of moulds and yeasts, whereas those soaked in a chlorine bleach solution allowed a frighteningly higher percentage to survive. It makes you think, doesn't it?

It is also important to keep things clean when filling bottles and jars.

Filling Jars and Bottles

There is much written regarding the correct way to wash and clean thoroughly any containers to be used for storing chutneys and pickles. However, it seems to be generally accepted that this is best done by placing them in boiling water (but you will need to take care in preventing the jars and bottles from banging together and weakening or even cracking during their hot bath), then into the oven at 120°C for twenty minutes. Another method is to place your jars into a cold oven and turn the temperature to 160°C (325°F), turning off the heat just as soon as the temperature is reached, but leaving the jars in situ until they have cooled down and are ready to fill. Other successful chutney and pickle makers suggest just running them through the dishwasher cycle, saying that they'll be sterilized whilst drying.

Microwaves can, of course, be very useful in sterilizing jars prior to packing with chutneys, pickles and relishes. Fill clean jars one-quarter full of water and bring to a full boil. Remove and pour out the water before leaving the jars to dry upside-down on a wire rack. Note that the jars will not all come to the boil at the same time and that they should *always* be removed from the microwave using oven gloves.

Whatever you are bottling, always ensure that the necks of the receptacles are most carefully wiped clean after filling. Moulds will grow on most things – including the tops of pickles – and are not much discouraged by acidity, especially if there is air around. Use cleaned, warm jars and fill to leave about 2.5cm/1in headspace above the pickles.

Cover and seal the jars at once (unless a particular recipe states otherwise). If merely pickling or bottling vegetables or fruit, top up the vinegar levels until all of the ingredients are completely covered, otherwise they will be in danger of becoming discoloured. Tops must be airtight, or the vinegar will dry out. For fruit pickles, keep a little surplus sweetened vinegar in reserve so that you can top up as necessary (some fruits absorb the vinegar as they mature).

For chutneys, fill the jars until above the shoulder and certainly to within 1.5cm/½in of the top, taking care to tap the chutney down gently with the back of a spoon in order to reduce and eliminate any air bubbles. Sealing is crucial and can be simply done by spooning in the hot chutney – the steam of which creates its own vacuum.

For ketchups, fill clean, dry, warm bottles to within 2.5cm/1in of the top and seal immediately. Sauces made from ingredients with a low acid content, such as ripe tomatoes and mushrooms, must be sterilized after bottling – this prevents fermentation during storage.

STERILIZING KETCHUP

If the bottles are sealed with screw tops, tighten them, then give them a half turn back. If they are sealed with corks, tie them down to prevent them from blowing out. Using a deep saucepan, make a false bottom of folded newspaper and stand the prepared bottles on it. Make sure that none of the bottles are touching one another, using small pieces of newspaper or kitchen roll to separate them if necessary. Add sufficient cold water to reach the bottom of the corks or screw tops. Heat the water to 77°C/170°F. If you do not have a thermometer, heat slowly until tiny bubbles are rising continually from the bottom of the pan — this might take about an hour. Keep the water at this heat for a further half an hour before removing the bottles, tightening the screw tops, then rubbing a thin film of paraffin wax over each cork or bottle top in order to provide a truly airtight seal.

STORAGE

Sterilized ketchups will keep for several months and can be opened and reopened during that time, but it is important to use unsterilized ketchups quite quickly after being opened. Pickles and chutneys vary in the time they need to be kept before they can be eaten and much depends on what exactly you are intending to store. Mary Hart says that vegetable chutney is more 'stable' than one made of fruit in terms of keeping – and as she has won countless awards, in addition to coming 'best in show' out of 581 entries in a national competition recently, she should know! Generally though, chutneys, especially highly spiced, thick ones, will improve in taste and texture by being kept for at least three months and certainly up to a year before use, although, as will be seen from the recipes, some are ready to eat almost as soon as they are made. A few types of pickles will improve for up to two, or even three years, but all reach an optimum point and then deteriorate. The aficionados reckon that chutneys and pickles are at their best nine to twelve months after bottling, so,

Once opened, it is probably best to store chutneys and ketchups in the fridge.

unlike jams and similar preserves seen at autumn horticultural shows, which may well have been made from the current season's fruit, chutneys and pickles that stand the best chance of coming away with a first prize are quite likely to have been made the previous year.

If you have a traditional larder, they are undoubtedly the best places in which to store any sealed chutneys, pickles and relishes, but even the most clinical of modern kitchens must have a tiny corner or cupboard that is cool, dark, dry and capable of storing a few jars and bottles. Chutney and pickle maker Lynn Brodie suggests that, where possible, you should store your jars of produce in cardboard boxes against an outside wall, but in a room that is damp-proof. Never store any preserves near hot pipes, radiators or the household boiler. Nor should you consider the loft unless it is well insulated in the actual roof space and there is no danger of freezing (whilst accidental freezing itself will not cause any problems to effectively sealed jars and their contents, freezing and thawing might possibly affect the consistency). If boxes of chutneys and pickles do have to be kept in an outhouse or similar, cover the boxes with wads of newspapers and/or old (clean) blankets.

Before consuming, check the jar and examine the lid for tightness and vacuum. Hold it up to the light and make sure that there is no evidence of the contents having leaked and dried around the top of the jar – which could very well suggest that a seal has not been effective and that the contents may have spoiled as a result. Once a jar has been opened, it is nowadays recommended that it be kept in the fridge. When we were all growing up, five-year-old chutneys and pickles would be pulled from the back of the cupboard and we would eat them with no apparent ill-effects. Neither did sauces such as ketchup seem to be kept in the fridge once opened. Oil, vinegar and sugar are preservatives and any spices are an added bonus in helping to kill bacteria, or at least to stop fungal growth. So, once opened, do we really need to keep that part finished bottle or jar in the fridge? Logic says not, but modern thinking suggests that we perhaps should!

Choosing the Right Ingredients

There is a world of difference between the commercially produced chutneys, pickles and relishes that are so often found on the supermarket shelves and the homemade delights tucked away on the shelves of the enthusiast's larder. Put simply, the basic difference is that, in the one lovingly prepared in the kitchen, you can taste and identify the actual ingredients. The reason why is also simple. As head chef Jonathan Waters says, 'The ingredients of homemade chutney are chopped by hand, whereas commercial products are machine prepared – and that surely, misses the point of individuality?' Chutney and jam expert Lynn Brodie believes much the same thing and adds, 'If you have a passion for what you're creating, you'll end up with a good quality product far better than anything that can be produced commercially.' As an aside to this, although chopping fruit and vegetables by hand is long and laborious, it does, according to those who know about these things, give a considerably better texture in the end than if using a food processor.

Much as we'd all like to be self-sufficient (and would there be anything to be more proud of than producing a whole batch of goods, the ingredients of which we have either grown in the garden or collected from the wild?), there is, unfortunately, the very real prospect of having to source much of our, quite literally raw, materials from supermarkets, pick-your-owns, or the local farmers' market. Whilst there is nothing intrinsically wrong with that, a greater part of the excitement of preparing any chutney, pickle or relish is in adhering to the mantra that whatever you use, must, wherever possible, be seasonal. If, for example, you see a ripe cauliflower in your garden, or at your farmers' market at the end of summer, as opposed to an imported one at the supermarket in February, then you will surely know that it is time to start making piccalilli.

BASIC INGREDIENTS

It is important, when pickling or spicing vegetables or fruit, that they are of top quality. For pickling, most vegetables are first washed and then salted, or soaked in brine. Granny would have always insisted that block, rather than packet, salt was used, but it may be quite difficult to find nowadays. She would also have told you that it is important to

Growing your own vegetables makes the whole experience of cooking pickles and chutneys all the more pleasurable.

use the best quality vinegar available, because it is only then that the correct amount of acetic acid content will keep the vegetables as they should be – in fact, if you want to get really technical, use only the best vinegar that has an acetic acid content of at least 5 per cent.

Vinegar

Vinegar is a preservative for pickling – if you *cook* anything in vinegar, it then becomes a chutney! You can buy ready-spiced vinegar, but it is easy to make in the kitchen and gives you a little more flexibility due to the fact that you can vary the amounts of spices added in order to suit your own taste. 'Ordinary' malt vinegar is commonly used in situations where colour is not important and is traditionally favoured for the pickling of onions and shallots, but distilled, or white, malt vinegar is thought to give a better flavour in other recipes and will actually enhance the colour of pickled produce. According to Lynn Brodie, Sarson's vinegar works well, but with supermarket own brands, it is a matter of trial and error. Cider or good wine vinegar is often used for making fruit-based pickles and can be used in many relishes. Where cider vinegar is used in chutneys, remember that it has a stronger taste and may need simmering for longer – it is, however, most suitable for the sweeter chutneys and it gives more of a 'body'. Try using balsamic vinegar when pickling blackberries.

Vinegar is one of the most important ingredients in making chutneys and pickles (as are onions and garlic)

MAKING YOUR OWN SPICED VINEGAR

Many books advise preparing your own spiced vinegar at least two months before you need it.

To each 1.2ltr/2pt of vinegar, add 30g/1oz of mixed pickling spice. Or add 7g/¼oz each of the following spice mixture: cloves, mace, allspice and cinnamon, together with a few peppercorns and one or two small pieces of dry root ginger. Leave to infuse for several weeks, during which time the bottles should be shaken occasionally in order to prevent the spices from sinking to the bottom. Strain before use – alternatively, to prevent having to do the latter, tie the spices into a muslin bag and hang it in the vinegar.

If life is too hectic to think several weeks ahead and spiced vinegar is required immediately, all is not lost, as an 'instant' version can be made as follows:

- Put the vinegar and spices in a basin and place the basin in a pan of cold water. The water should be halfway up the basin.
- Cover the basin with a lid or plate and bring the water to the boil.
- Take the saucepan from the heat and let it stand until the vinegar is cold. Strain to remove the spices before use.

SALT

If too little salt is used in chutneys, they can ferment and smell, apart from being an obvious health risk. Chef Jonathan Waters recommends using sea salt because it is not so 'harsh' – it is non-iodized and, as such, will not discolour or darken your major vegetable and fruit components. Salt aficionados suggest that French sea salt (famously taken from the country's north-west coast) has a much softer and fresher flavour than that found anywhere else, but we think that might be taking things to unnecessary extremes in our quest for perfect ingredients. Incidentally, remember that salt is a mineral, so, provided that you are moderately sensible in where you store it, it can be kept indefinitely without any danger of going stale. Alternatively, use LoSalt, for health reasons.

BRINING

In some recipes vegetables such as onions and cauliflowers need to be salted, or 'brined', before being pickled. The reason for doing so is to reduce the moisture content and retain the vegetable's crispness. Try either of the following ways:

- soak the vegetables in 2.5ltr/4pt water into which 225g/8oz coarse salt has been dissolved
- alternatively, spread a layer of the prepared vegetables on a large dish and sprinkle liberally with salt (add other layers of vegetables if necessary, sprinkling each with salt).

Marinades, pickles and brines are, according to Tom Stobart in *The Cook's Encyclopaedia* (Batsford, 1980), 'aromatized liquids into which food is put for various purposes. A brine always has salt as its most important ingredient . . . a pickle may be a brine or it may be based on vinegar, lemon juice or any other sour fruit juice, or verjuice (the juice of unripe fruit, sometimes concentrated by boiling) and is also a preservative'. (*See also* 'Marinades' in Chapter 5.)

SUGAR

Sugar types may vary from recipe to recipe, but, more often than not, they seem to call for soft, light brown sugar. However, unless a recipe states differently, it is usually a safe bet to use granulated (which is always useful to have as part of the basic essentials of any cook's store cupboard). Brown sugar is normally used to give a good flavour and a dark, rich colour to chutneys and relishes. But use demerara or white if preferred, or if you want a light colour to your pickles – white vinegar and white sugar help to keep the bright colour of red tomato chutney or ketchup, for example. Whilst on the subject of sweetness and colour, it is worthwhile to note that, generally, the riper any fruit and vegetables are, the more natural sugars they will contain, plus they will give the finished product more colour.

SPICES

Cayenne, cinnamon (sticks), cloves, mace and mustard (sometimes in its seed form) are all mentioned regularly in our recipes, as are ground cumin, curry powder, allspice berries and sachets of mixed spices. As for pepper, well, it seems there is only one kind as far as most are concerned and that is the aromatic black peppercorn. Keep the peppercorns whole unless it is recommended otherwise, in which case grind them as needed by the use of a wooden peppermill, or pound them with a pestle and mortar. Whole white (and indeed, pink) peppercorns are available, but seem to be rarely used by the professionals.

Whether chilli peppers are technically a spice or not, they are an essential component of many a recipe and fresh ones should be selected, bearing in mind the adage that the smaller the pepper, the hotter its contents are likely to be. Dried examples include anchos, arols and probably the most used of all, cayenne. Commercially ground chilli will lose some of its efficaciousness over a period of time and so, where appropriate, try to buy whole chillis (many recipes will call for them to be included whole anyway), then crush them in a pestle and mortar, or small coffee grinder, as required. It is, however, worth considering removing the inner membranes and seeds unless you wish to achieve something that is exceptionally hot. Remember that ground spices will make vinegar go cloudy, so if it's important that your pickles be attractively presented (and why should they not? It is as easy to make a clean, colourful-looking pickle as it is one that has the appearance of being made with last evening's washing-up water), always use whole spices. Fresh root ginger is normally grated before being added to any recipe. Ground ginger

A pestle and mortar is useful when a recipe calls for spices to be ground or cracked.

Chillies are included in many recipes and can also be used to flavour oils.

does, however, have its place in some recipes, but in green tomato chutney, for example, many enthusiasts recommend using root ginger.

Mary Hart suggests that tamarind can make an interesting addition to many recipes, but warns against including the seeds. She also suggests using coriander in some recipes (as may be seen in several of her contributions that feature in the main part of this book). Creating new recipes is a question of being intuitive, employing trial and error and the ability to 'think outside the box'. It is also worth experimenting by substituting the spices given in the recipes for others – it is, however, best to try a 'taste-test' first: if, for example, you are making apple chutney, try sprinkling a small amount of spice onto a slice of fresh apple and see how it works in the mouth.

OILS

Oils will only ever be required for relishes. Personally, we prefer to use good quality virgin olive oil for virtually everything, but others have, alongside their standard bottle of olive oil, one containing perhaps sesame or the beautifully flavoured walnut and hazel-nut oils. Always buy the best you can and store it in a dark place away from the heat of the hob. Although oils are more likely to be used as an addition to relishes rather than chutneys, it will, of course, be necessary to soften or fry off ingredients such as onions before they are included in a chutney. For this, there is little point in using anything other than decent, but nevertheless basic, olive oil, although on occasion (when, for instance, a higher temperature is needed), sunflower oil might serve equally as well – as would groundnut oil.

Flavoured Oils

When making flavoured oils for use in relishes, it is usually simply a case of adding herbs or spices to a bottle and filling it with oil in order that the herbs will be infused. When including other things – chillis, for example – it may be necessary to heat the oil (to a temperature of around 180°C/350°F) before pouring it into the jar or bottle. This does, however, have the benefit of ensuring that there is little likelihood of the chillis encouraging botulism spores, as well as usefully speeding up the infusion process.

PICKLING LIME

Although none of the recipes included within this book calls for the use of pickling lime, we thought that, in order to dispel any possible confusion, mention at least ought to be made of its existence. There is a huge difference between the ingredient 'pickling lime' and the action of 'pickling limes' – lime in this context being that derived from limestone or other minerals heavy in calcium content. It was known to have been used by the Aztec tribes of northern and central Mexico, who used it alongside readily available spices to help preserve vegetables and fruit.

Pickling lime mixture, basically calcium hydroxide, can be bought from some of the more specialized purveyors of preserving suppliers and is included in some pickling methods because of the fact that it firms the texture of any vegetables being used. Because of its naturally occurring alkalinity, it is, however, extremely important that all the lime residue is thoroughly washed off the vegetables before pickling proper can begin, the lime having the effect of neutralizing vinegar or any other acids necessary to keep produce safely.

Pickling Limes

Having briefly mentioned above the act of pickling limes, we thought that it may be of interest to include verbatim a typical pickling limes recipe taken from Eliza Acton's 1845 book *Modern Cookery for Private Families*:

> Wipe eight fine sound limes very clean, and make, at equal distances, four deep incisions in each, from the stalk to the blossom end, but without dividing the fruit; stuff them with as much salt as they will contain, lay them into a deep dish, and place them in a sunny window, or in some warm place for a week or ten days, keeping them often turned and basted with their own liquor; then rub them with some good plain turmeric, and put them with their juice, into a stone jar with a small head of garlic, divided into cloves and peeled, and a dozen small onions stuck with twice as many cloves. Boil in two quarts of white wine vinegar, half a pound of ginger slightly

bruised, two ounces of whole black pepper, and half a pound of mustard seed; take them from the fire and pour them directly on the limes; cover the jar with a plate, and let them remain until the following day, then add to the pickle half a dozen capsicums and tie a skin and a fold of thick paper over the jar.

FRUITS AND VEGETABLES

To make the best chutneys, pickles and relishes, it is necessary to choose fruits and vegetables that are fresh and preferably free of rot or blemishes – bruised fruit will ferment, which you do *not* want. Having said that, it would be a shame not to use what nature (or a kind neighbour) provides and so, if it is decided to use windfalls, be sure to cut out any obviously bruised sections and use only that which is sound – for that reason, it may pay to increase the weights of windfalls given in the recipe to be sure of ending up with the correct amount of prepared fruit. Where a recipe mentions lemons and/or limes, buy unwaxed ones whenever possible and, if you cannot, scrub waxed ones well before use.

Tomatoes should generally be as ripe as possible before being included in a recipe – if necessary, allow them to ripen on a sunny windowsill (but be careful that they do not dry out), or try storing them in cardboard or wooden boxes in a cool, moderately humid room. As a direct alternative, try covering the boxes with newspaper, as tomatoes will also ripen in complete darkness. To speed up the ripening process put a ripening tomato,

Use unwaxed lemons whenever possible.

'Sweating' and preparing onions for inclusion in onion marmalade chutney.

apple or banana in the box. Fruit and vegetables can come from the greengrocer's, farmers' market, the vegetable plot or the hedgerow.

Vegetables particularly suitable for pickling include beetroot, shallots, cabbage (green and red), cauliflower, courgettes and aubergines. Cook them slowly, as the recipes dictate, in order to impart the dark colour and rich, gentle taste so typical of a good chutney or pickle. Soften onions and any other tough vegetables by cooking them gently in a little water in a covered pan.

From Field and Hedgerow

When using ingredients from the hedgerow, their collection will, of course, be very seasonal indeed. Take great care when harvesting mushrooms as, excellent though they may be (in the year 800BC, Homer described them as being the fruit of the union between heaven and earth), many of the several thousand varieties found throughout the world are poisonous. Knowing how to tell them apart is an art that requires dedication and study, so before using any that you have found double-check them and throw away any of which you are not 100 per cent sure. If you are using a book to help with naming, make sure that it is one illustrated with clear photographs and not with paintings or line drawings, as this will make for a far more accurate and positive identification. Mushrooms are a delicate food that rot quickly and do not conserve their properties for more than forty-eight hours. Furthermore, it is important to avoid picking mushrooms

Aim to use any hedgerow fruit as soon as possible – although some, such as blackberries, can be frozen until such time as you can begin preparing your chutneys and relishes.

from near the road because they very soon absorb any toxic substances. It is also useful to remember the golden rule of thumb for mushroom picking, which is never to pull them but to cut them carefully with a knife.

It is far more likely that most of what you will find growing for free in the countryside will be fruits and berries, and therefore perhaps better suited to jams and preserves. There are, nevertheless, several inspiring recipes for chutneys and relishes made from hedgerows in the main section of this book. Choose ripe fruits that are deep coloured and not blemished by green or hard brown patches. Once you have taken your fruit home, rinse it thoroughly in water and store it in a fridge for no longer than three days. Ideally, aim to use the fruit as soon as possible, although some, such as blackberries and elderberries, can be frozen until such time as you can begin preparing your chutneys. If you are on the coast, look out for wild samphire, which can be pickled.

Dried Fruits
Whilst we and others continually advise that, where possible, you should use seasonal fruits and vegetables – after all, that's the whole essence of chutneys, pickles and relishes – some dried fruits can work well in chutneys. Sultanas and raisins are obvious candidates (and supermarket own brands are good enough), but for an extra taste of unexpected sweetness, try including dried apricots or dates in some of your recipes.

Onions and garlic are among the most common vegetables used in chutney, pickle and relish making.

SUITABLE CROPS FROM THE GARDEN

Of course, the basic idea behind making chutneys and the like is to use up seasonal produce of which there might be a glut: preserving sits far more easily on the mind than does wastage. However, the practice and joys of making some of the recipes that appear in this book may mean that you begin to grow crops specifically for turning into chutneys, pickles and relishes! A brief list, together with their basic requirements might, as a result, prove useful.

Onions and Shallots
By far the most common ingredient of any recipe is onions. They are so versatile and a staple of any cooking. The unfortunate thing is that in order to have sufficient for year-round use, a fair-sized vegetable plot is required. Where space permits, give it a go. Grow both onions and shallots from sets – it is so much easier than attempting to do so from seed, as they take less time to mature and seem to cope better in the colder areas of

the country. They are also less likely to be attacked by onion fly. The best pickled 'onions' are, in fact, shallots and the sets you buy for growing will be full-sized, but will multiply once planted by the simple expedient of producing clusters of 'new' shallots from the original bulb.

Garlic

Like shallots, garlic produces more garlic from the original parent plant. Although many gardeners will tell you not to do so (advising you instead to buy from a gardening cata-logue or garden centre), it is possible to grow garlic very simply by taking a bulb bought from the supermarket or farmers' market and splitting it into individual cloves before planting them in well-drained soil at a depth of about 5cm/2in and about 15cm/6in apart. Weed and water in dry weather and, if planted in March, your garlic should be ready for use by August – just in time for the main pickling and chutney making season.

Tomatoes

Outdoor tomatoes will, if you choose the right type, do well enough in an average summer for you to enjoy ripe ones on your salads as well as being able to make a few jars of red tomato chutney and bottles of ketchup – and the inevitable green ones that have failed to ripen by summer's end can be used in green tomato chutney, a recipe for which can be found in the next chapter. Buy them as plants from your local garden centre, or grow them in pots in the house before planting them out in a sunny, sheltered spot. To keep the main plant growing strongly, nip out the little side shoots that will appear in the 'crux' between the leaf-bearing stems and the main stem. Once the first trusses of green fruit begin to form, it will be necessary to start giving the plants a liquid feed.

Courgettes

Courgettes are really only small marrows and similar growing conditions are required for both. Plant the seeds in pots early in the year (about March time) and bring them on in a greenhouse or on a sunny window ledge – in this way, they will be ready for plant-ing out once all the risk of frost has gone (belonging as they do to the cucumber family, courgettes are not hardy and are best planted in a sunny spot protected from strong winds) and you should be able to start using them much earlier than your neighbours. They need neither peeling nor seeding for inclusion in pickles and chutneys.

Beetroot

Beetroot is relatively easy to grow provided that you don't either over or under water, in which case it is likely that the roots will be hard and/or 'split'. Harvesting for pickling should be done when the roots of the globe varieties are not much bigger than a golf ball. Wash the beetroots, being careful not to break the skin, trim the leaves, but not too close to the 'neck', and place in a pan containing just enough boiling (salted) water to cover the roots properly. Simmer for about one and a half hours, or until the beetroot feels soft when the point of a knife is inserted. Allow to cool, then remove the skin and 'top and tail'. Cut into slices, place in suitable (clean and sterilized) jars and cover with pickling vinegar before sealing and storing.

Cherry tomatoes can be grown outdoors and are every bit as useful in chutney making as those of a 'normal' size.

Carrots

Carrots are an important part of several recipes in this book. They add colour, texture and a certain sweetness and, if space in the garden permits, should be considered for growing. There are, in fact, several short-rooted varieties that are useful for either container growing, or for heavy soils (although most carrot types thrive best in light, sandy soil). Grow them in full sun and give them plenty of water. Normally they are prepared for chutney and pickle making by being scraped and cut into small chunks, although there are occasions when they may require grating or being cut into long, thin slivers.

Cauliflowers

An essential ingredient of piccalilli, cauliflowers need consolidated and carefully prepared soil to grow well and produce healthy heads of florets. A sunny spot is required and, to prevent small, straggly heads, they need plenty of watering. Although it might be easier to buy plants ready for transferring straight into your garden, cauliflowers are, nevertheless, easy enough to grow from seed planted either in trays in the greenhouse, or directly in the soil where they will need thinning and eventually transplanting into their permanent positions. It is also possible to buy cauliflower seeds of a miniature type (sometimes described in the seed catalogues as 'baby' vegetables), which can be quite advantageous in the small garden as they require less space in which to grow.

Carrots add colour, texture and a certain piquancy to many chutneys and pickles.

Herbs

Herbs can be grown in the minimal amount of space and, because you rarely require a vast amount at any one time will, if you are careful in what you choose, supply you with frequent and adequate 'harvests'. As many of them come from Mediterranean regions, in order to do really well they will require well-drained soil and a sunny, but sheltered, position in the garden. Types suitable for the chutney and pickle maker include coriander (a hardy annual), fennel, thyme (a strong-growing perennial) and dill (sown in succession from spring onwards). Bay is a herb, but, unlike the majority of herbs, is very slow growing. Plant it in a suitably sized pot so that, in the autumn, it can be moved to a more sheltered position (or indoors in the conservatory perhaps?) for the winter months.

Eggs

Not fruit or vegetables, or even herbs; eggs are, however, quite likely to be found in the chicken run at the end of the garden. At certain times, it might just so happen that there is a glut of them and there is a limit as to how much time one can put aside in order to make cakes or desserts to go in the freezer. Neighbours, whilst generally glad to take some eggs off your hands, might even start hiding when they see you heading towards them with yet another box, so you need to think of other things to do with them! If you like them, pickling eggs is a good way of ensuring that nothing goes to waste.

Bantam eggs are particularly good in this context, although it is interesting to note some advice given in a letter which appeared in *Smallholder* magazine, the gist of which

The perfect kitchen garden from which all manner of pickles and chutneys can be made.

concerned the suitability of fresh eggs for pickling. Experience has apparently taught the letter writer that home-produced eggs boiled for pickling are difficult to peel before being put into vinegar because they are too fresh; unless they are old, the shell will not remove easily and as a result some of the egg tends to come away with the shell. This not only makes them look unattractive, but also runs the risk of the contents of the yolk leaking through into the vinegar, causing it to go cloudy. For this reason, the writer recommended leaving home-produced eggs to 'mature' before using them.

Recipes for Characterful Chutneys

There is no secret art to making chutneys and, although you should stick to the proportions given in the recipes, it is possible to alter the flavouring to your own taste. Don't be tempted into doubling or even trebling the quantities given and making huge vats of a certain recipe until you've tried it in the amounts given here – just because the authors like a particular recipe doesn't mean that you necessarily will and a huge cauldron of personally unpalatable chutney is obviously a waste of time and valuable ingredients. Any recipes for particularly sweet ones should be undercooked, rather than overcooked, because they will go on softening as the ingredients cool. Most recipes call for long, gentle simmering, a process that will undoubtedly give the best results; it is important not to become impatient and try to do things too quickly, otherwise you will merely end up with a finished product that tastes burnt. Stir more frequently as the chutney cooks and the liquid evaporates.

The numbers of jars that the recipes will fill obviously varies depending on the volume, types of fruits and vegetables used and the consistency of the finished product. The size of the jar or bottle chosen also has some relevance – and as we mention elsewhere, it is important to have a few small, odd-sized jars and bottles on hand in which to store that odd spoonful of chutney that always seems to be left in the bottom of the pan!

TESTING

To test when a chutney is ready, tilt the saucepan and draw a wooden spoon through the mixture. It should leave a clean path in the bottom of the pan, with no traces of liquid – Mary Hart describes it as being like the time when Moses divided the Red Sea during the exodus from Egypt, which was, according to Biblical references, made by the Israelites into the Promised Land; a quite appropriate analogy in the circumstances!

It had been our original intention to have a separate section dealing with chutneys (and relishes) made from ingredients foraged from the countryside, but this has proved to be an impossible task because the definition of truly 'wild' food can sometimes be so difficult. Elderberries are no problem, but what of blackberries, which can also be cultivated in the garden, or windfall apples that are possible to collect as crab apples from a tree-lined hedge as well as specific varieties from the orchard?

Fresh Pear Chutney

It is not always necessary to make vast vats of chutneys or pickles and spend all day boiling and bottling. Sometimes all that's needed to lift a quite ordinary recipe is the inclusion of a spoonful or two of chutney made whilst the main course is cooking. Fresh Pear Chutney is just such a recipe and goes well with venison in particular.

2 pears	1 cinnamon stick
1 small chilli, deseeded and chopped	pinch of ground cloves
1 clove garlic, peeled and crushed	55g/2oz sugar
1 small piece of ginger, grated	2 tablespoons apple cider vinegar

Make the pear chutney by peeling, coring and roughly chopping two pears. Put these, together with the other ingredients, into a small pan and cook gently until the sugar has dissolved.

Simmer until the pears are soft (about fifteen minutes).

Fresh Pear Chutney.

West Country Pear Chutney

Perfect with a good chunk of mature Cheddar cheese as part of a Ploughman's Lunch, West Country Pear Chutney will keep for two to three months in the larder and, in fact, storing will intensify and improve the flavour. If you are keeping with the West Country theme and not intending to do too much in the afternoon, then try accompanying your lunch with a bottle of Badger Poacher's Choice ale. Made by family brewers Hall & Woodhouse based in Blandford St Mary, Dorset, its robust, subtly fruity flavours combine well with game, desserts and mature cheeses.

2kg/4lb 6oz pears, peeled, cored and roughly chopped
1kg/2lb 3oz onions, peeled and finely chopped
1 clove of garlic, peeled and crushed
sachet of pickling spice (or 30g/1oz of same, tied tightly into a small piece of muslin)

350g/12oz caster sugar
600ml/1pt cider vinegar
2 teaspoons turmeric
30g/1oz cornflour

Place the pears, onions, garlic and pickling spice into a heavy-bottomed (or preserving) pan and cook over a low heat, stirring gently so as to ensure that no ingredients stick.

Once the pears have formed a purée and the onions have softened, stir in the sugar until it has dissolved. Taste the mixture and add more sugar if too tart for your liking.

Add the vinegar, stirring gently all the time. Bring to the boil, then simmer for five minutes before spooning out and throwing away the sachet/bag of pickling spice. Mix the turmeric and the cornflour with a little water to make a paste and add to the chutney.

Bring to the boil again, stirring until it thickens even more (if the chutney appears runnier than desired at the point of removing the pickling spices, double the quantity of cornflour added to the turmeric).

Spoon into five clean, sterilized and normal-sized jam jars, sealing the lids whilst the chutney is still hot.

Gooseberry Chutney

Mary Hart says that the essential difference between a commercially produced chutney and one which is made in your own kitchen is that in the latter you can taste and identify the actual fruit! Here's a recipe of hers that offers a solution of what to do with all the gooseberries in the garden once you have had your fill of gooseberry pie!

1.5kg/3lb 5oz gooseberries, topped and tailed
225g/8oz onions, peeled and chopped
300ml/10fl oz water
500g/1lb 2oz white sugar
1 tablespoon ground ginger

2 teaspoons salt
½ teaspoon cayenne pepper
½ teaspoon dried garlic flakes
1 whole cinnamon stick
600ml/1pt white malt vinegar

Oranges, whether they be used whole, sliced, or just the rind or juice, are used with regularity in a great many chutney and relish recipes.

Place the gooseberries in a preserving pan together with the chopped onion and water. Cook very gently until soft and pulpy.

Stir in the sugar, spices and dried garlic flakes; add the vinegar, stirring gently all the time. Still stirring, turn the heat up until the mixture is almost, but not quite, boiling. Reduce the heat and simmer the mixture, cooking gently for about two hours, or until thick.

Remove the cinnamon stick, pour into warm jars; seal, label and store for at least six weeks before eating.

Rhubarb and Orange Chutney

A recipe from the excellent *Farmhouse Kitchen II* cookery book first published in 1978 (*see* also Apple, Onion and Mint Pickle). It was submitted for this book by Doreen Allars, Welbourn, Lincolnshire.

900g/2lb rhubarb (weighed after trimming)
3 onions
2 oranges
450g/1lb raisins
900g/2lb demerara sugar

850ml/1½pt malt vinegar
1 tablespoon mustard seed
1 tablespoon white peppercorns
1 level teaspoon powdered allspice

Wash and wipe the rhubarb before cutting it into short pieces and putting it into a preserving pan or large saucepan. Peel and chop the onions and add them to the pan. Finely shred the rind from the oranges, squeeze out the juice and discard the pith. Add to the pan.

Add the raisins, sugar and vinegar. In a square of muslin, tie the three spices and place this in the pan. Bring to the boil and simmer gently until thick.

Place clean preserving jars into a very cool oven (110°C/225°F) and warm them thoroughly.

Remove the spice bag from the mixture and fill the warmed jars nearly to the brim with hot chutney. Put vinegar-proof lids on at once. Label and date the jars. Store in a cool, dark place. Let it mature for three months before eating.

Rapid Rhubarb Chutney

Another quick chutney (*see also* Fresh Pear Chutney above) is this one, a 450g/1lb jar of which can be created in about half an hour. Not only does it go well with ham, lamb, duck and cheese, but, unusually for a chutney, is also perfect when placed alongside smoked mackerel or a freshly caught, simply grilled trout.

450g/1lb rhubarb, trimmed, washed and
    roughly sliced
1 medium onion, peeled and finely chopped
100ml/3fl oz cider vinegar or white wine
    vinegar

1cm/½in piece fresh ginger, finely chopped
    or grated
200g/7oz sugar
½ teaspoon salt

Heat the onion, vinegar, ginger, sugar and salt in a heavy-bottomed pan. Bring to a rolling boil (a very fast boil that doesn't slow when stirred) for about five minutes, then add the rhubarb. Reduce the heat until the mixture has slightly thickened and, if the chutney is intended for immediate use (for use with smoked mackerel, for example), allow it to cool until it is just warm. If storing, spoon into the jar whilst still hot.

Wakefield Rhubarb Chutney

Many professional Yorkshire-based chefs use rhubarb in their recipes. The main ingredient is very seasonal and the best is produced within the county – the area around Wakefield being variously known as either the 'Rhubarb Triangle', or the 'Rhubarb Capital of the World'!

900g/2lb rhubarb, washed and chopped
2 lemons
900g/2lb brown sugar
450/1lb sultanas
1 onion, peeled and finely chopped

600ml/1pt malt vinegar
1 teaspoon ground ginger
1 teaspoon salt
1 teaspoon cayenne pepper

Grate the rind and squeeze the juice of the lemons into a heavy-bottomed pan before adding the rest of the ingredients. Bring to the boil, then lower the heat until the contents are simmering gently. Stir periodically until the vinegar has been absorbed and the mixture has thickened and darkened in colour. Cool and place in warm jars, but allow the chutney to grow cold before sealing and storing.

Fat Olives' Chutney

Laurence Murphy of *Fat Olives*, Emsworth, Hampshire, kindly give us this recipe.

6 firm Conference pears, peeled, cored and diced
2 Bramley apples, peeled, cored and diced
2 onions, peeled and finely chopped
225g/8oz castor sugar
125ml/4fl oz balsamic vinegar
1 tablespoon black treacle

½ teaspoon ground nutmeg
1 tablespoon pink peppercorns
3 cloves
1 bay leaf
salt and pepper

Place all the ingredients into a large, heavy-bottomed pan over a low heat and cook slowly until the mixture feels soft and is thick in texture.

Remove the bay leaf (and the cloves if you can find them!), taste and, if felt necessary, add a little more sugar and/or vinegar until it is to your personal liking. Season with the salt and pepper – turning it thoroughly into the mixture – before placing the chutney into sterilized Kilner jars.

Apple and Pear Chutney with Stilton cheese.

Apple and Pear Chutney

Mary Hart was kind enough to offer this little gem, saying that it's 'sweet, but sour, hot and also cool'. Sounds intriguing and, as such, just cries out to be made!

1.25kg/2lb12oz pears and apples, peeled,
   cored and chopped
500g/1lb 2oz onions, peeled and chopped
225g/8oz chopped dates
Rind and juice of a lemon
Rind and juice of an orange

300ml/10fl oz malt vinegar
½ teaspoon ground cloves
½ teaspoon ground ginger
Salt to taste
225g/8oz brown sugar

Place the pears and apples together with all the other ingredients (except the sugar) into a preserving pan and simmer gently until all the fruit is really tender. Add the sugar and continue cooking until the mixture is really thick.

Pot into warm, sterile jars, seal and label.

Goosnargh Orange and Lemon Chutney

The little village of Goosnargh in Lancashire has no end to its culinary talents! This local recipe for Orange and Lemon Chutney accompanies the duck of the region and also goes well with goose and cold ham slices.

2 oranges, washed and scrubbed
3 lemons, ditto
450g/1lb cooking apples
450g/1lb sugar
450ml/16fl oz white wine vinegar
1 blade mace
1 cinnamon stick

1in/2.5cm piece fresh root ginger, roughly scraped
1 teaspoon whole cloves
a few peppercorns
225g/8oz onions, peeled and finely chopped
175g/6oz sultanas
salt and pepper

Halve the oranges and lemons and squeeze their juices into a bowl. Finely shred the peel and flesh (carefully discarding the pips). Add the peel and flesh to the bowl containing the juice and add the vinegar and all the spices. Mix together well and leave to stand for at least a day.

Place the mixture into a large chutney pan; peel, core and chop the apples and add to the pan, together with the onions. Cook very gently over a low heat until the fruit and onions are tender.

Remove the pan from the heat before stirring in the sultanas, sugar and a little salt and pepper to taste. Once the sugar appears to have dissolved, return to the heat and bring the contents of the pan to the boil. Reduce the heat and simmer gently for approximately one hour, or until the mixture is thick and all the juices absorbed.

As with almost all chutneys, pour into warm, sterilized jars and seal immediately.

Kent Windfall Chutney

As gardeners, there always seems to be more unripe green tomatoes left at the end of the growing season than one knows what to do with! It's always possible to make traditional green tomato chutney, but blending them with windfall plums, pears and apples to produce a chutney that works well with either cold meats or strong regional cheeses is, in our opinion, a far better idea!

1kg/2lb 3oz apples, peeled, cored and
    chopped into chunks of about 1.5cm (½in)
1kg/2lb 3oz pears, peeled, cored and
    chopped ditto
1kg/2lb 3oz plums, stoned
900g/2lb green tomatoes, washed and
    quartered
225g/8oz mixed seedless raisins and sultanas

450g/1lb marrow flesh, cut into small cubes
900g/2lb onions, peeled and chopped
850ml/1½pt malt vinegar
50g/2oz pickling spice (in sachets or tied into
    a corner of muslin to form a *bouquet garni*)
225g/8oz soft brown sugar
55g/2oz salt

Place the fruit, tomatoes, raisins and sultanas, marrow and onions into a large pan. Add half the amount of vinegar and the spices before bringing to the boil. Simmer until the ingredients are tender and pulpy in texture; occasionally stirring.

Add the sugar, salt and remainder of the vinegar, stirring continuously until the sugar has completely dissolved. Continue cooking over a low heat, giving the chutney an occasional stir until the mixture becomes thick – this may take up to two hours.

Once cooked, remove the spice bag(s), spoon into clean, sterilized jars and seal. Store for at least a month before using.

Walton Heath Blackberry Chutney

One of the best things about compiling a book of this nature is that you meet some very lovely people! Quite often it is as a result of a casual comment to someone and they then say 'Oh, I know someone who would most probably love to help.' Which is how we got to meet Lynn Brodie, who welcomed us into her house and, despite the fact that it was only 8.00am, had already prepared some perfect 'photo opportunities', as well as being kind enough to let us have this recipe and the recipe for Caribbean Chutney elsewhere in this chapter.

1kg/2lb 3oz blackberries
1kg/2lb 3oz dried ready-to-eat apricots
450g/1lb tinned crushed pineapples
225g/8oz sultanas
750g/1lb10oz onions, peeled and chopped
6 level teaspoons salt
1kg/2lb 3oz jam sugar (which includes pectin)
500ml/18fl oz cider vinegar

300ml/10fl oz malt vinegar
1kg/2lb 3oz soft light brown sugar
400g/14oz tomato puree
1 tablespoon ground pickling spices
2 tablespoons ground ginger
½ teaspoon cayenne pepper
½ teaspoon paprika

Walton Heath Chutney . . .

. . . and an autumnal view of Walton Heath, Surrey.

Simmer the chopped onions in both vinegars until softened and opaque. Add all the other ingredients and cook until the chutney is thick. Take care to stir the chutney regularly, especially later in the process once it becomes thicker, that is, every ten minutes to avoid it catching in the pan and burning; then every five minutes as it really thickens.

Once the mixture has reached a thick consistency, ladle it into hot, sterilized jars and seal with sterile lids.

Apple Chutney – Really Spicy

Another one of the excellent recipes kindly given to us by Mary Hart, this one is a spicy offering. If you prefer something a little milder, take a look at Mary's Apple Chutney – Mild and Fruity below.

2.5kg/5lb 8oz cooking apples, peeled, cored and diced
50g/1¾oz medium heat curry powder
30g/1oz mustard powder
1.5ltr/2½pt malt vinegar
1.2kg/2lb10oz onions, peeled and diced

55g/2oz garlic, peeled and crushed
450g/1lb sultanas
3 teaspoons allspice berries (tied in a muslin bag and crushed)
1.5kg/3lb 5oz demerara sugar

Mix the curry powder and mustard with a little of the vinegar and set aside.

Apple Chutney as made at home in the traditional way . . .

Place the apples, onions, garlic and sultanas in a preserving pan together with the rest of the vinegar and the spice bag. Bring to the boil, then cook gently for about an hour.

Now add the sugar, stirring all the time. Cook gently until starting to thicken, then add the curry powder/mustard mix. Simmer until thick and remove the spice bag.

Pot into warm, sterile jars, pressing the mixture down gently in order to remove any air pockets. Cover, label and store for two months before using.

Apple Chutney – Mild and Fruity

Another Mary Hart recipe – this one is a little less spicy than her Really Spicy Apple Chutney recipe above.

1.35kg/2lb10oz cooking apples, peeled cored and diced
1.35kg/2lb10oz onions, peeled and diced
450g/1lb sultanas
rind and juice of 2 lemons

4 tamarind pods (just the fleshy inside, not the husk or seeds)
600ml/1pt malt vinegar
675g/1lb 8oz demerara sugar

Put the apples, onions, sultanas, grated lemon rind, lemon juice and chopped tamarind flesh into a preserving pan, together with the vinegar, and bring to the boil, before turning down the heat and allowing all to cook gently until the apples and onions are tender.

. . . and making apple chutney on a commercial basis.

Add the sugar, stirring all the time. Cook slowly until thick.
Pot, label and store for several weeks before using.

Crab Apple Chutney

Crab apples can be found throughout the British countryside and they make a simple to prepare chutney that is a very good accompaniment to all manner of cold meats. It may be necessary to adjust the sugar quantities, depending on how 'sharp' you like your chutney.

2.25kg/5lb crab apples, peeled and cored
225g/8oz dates, stoned
115g/4oz raisins and/or sultanas
225g/8oz onions, peeled and minced
6 chillies, deseeded and chopped

450g/1lb demerara sugar
600ml/1pt vinegar
1 tablespoon salt
1 tablespoon powdered ginger

Place all the ingredients, together with a little of the vinegar, into a pan, bring to the boil and add more vinegar as required until all is absorbed. Stir well until the fruit is soft and the mixture is of a thick consistency.

Place in clean, warm jars, cool, seal and store.

Banana, Date and Mango

Although the main ingredients of this Mary Hart recipe are not likely to be sourced in the average UK kitchen garden, it is a somewhat exotic (and very tasty) addition to the chutneys and pickles store cupboard!

6 large ripe, but firm, bananas, sliced
350g/12oz stoned and chopped dates
450g/1lb mango flesh, chopped
450g/1lb apples, peeled, cored and chopped
350g/12oz soft brown sugar

1 hot chilli, chopped and deseeded
4 cloves garlic, peeled and chopped
2 teaspoons ground cinnamon
600ml/1pt malt vinegar
rind and juice of 1 lemon

Place all the ingredients in a preserving pan and cook over a gentle heat until the sugar has dissolved. Bring to the boil, then reduce the heat and simmer until thick, stirring now and then.

Pot into warm sterile jars; seal and label.

Australian Fig, Thyme and Raisin Chutney

The Country Women's Institute of Australia suggested and supplied this particular recipe. They say that it is popular amongst their members.

Banana, Date and Mango Chutney.

115g/4oz shallots, peeled and chopped
225g/8oz Spanish onions, peeled and chopped
450g/1lb fresh figs, chopped
115g/4oz 'golden' raisins

14g/½oz fresh thyme, very finely chopped
60ml/2fl oz rapeseed oil
30ml/1fl oz rice wine vinegar
salt and pepper, to taste

In a medium-sized saucepan, gently fry the shallots and onions in the oil until golden brown. Add the figs and raisins and immediately reduce the heat and cook for a minute or two – all the while stirring. Include the thyme and rice wine vinegar and cook for a further five minutes.

Season to taste, before cooling and refrigerating.

NB: As this recipe contains very little in the way of preserving agents, it will not keep and needs to be eaten within days.

Caribbean Chutney

The second of two recipes from Lynn Brodie. We just loved the idea of including something that could have come from the Caribbean and Lynn was happy to oblige with her unique recipe.

6 medium onions, peeled and chopped
1.2ltr/2pt malt vinegar
3kg/6lb 10oz ripe peeled large bananas
(allow 4kg/9lb before peeling – more
if bananas are small)
1kg/2lb 3oz seedless raisins
2 large Bramley cooking apples, peeled
and grated
3 level teaspoons salt

6 teaspoons medium heat curry powder
1 teaspoon medium heat chilli powder
3 yellow peppers
3 red peppers
8 large cloves garlic, peeled and crushed
3 teaspoons ground turmeric
½ teaspoon ground cloves
1.5kg/3lb 5oz soft light brown sugar
1 packet (sachet) coconut cream

Simmer chopped onions in vinegar till softened and opaque. Add mashed banana, raisins, grated cooking apple and bring to the boil, simmering for a few minutes.

Remove the pan from the heat. Add curry powder, chilli powder, chopped yellow and red peppers, crushed garlic, ground turmeric, ground cloves and salt. Slowly pour in the sugar, stirring continuously until the sugar is dissolved. Return the pan to the heat and stir until simmering to ensure all the sugar dissolves into the mixture and doesn't stick. Simmer gently and stir every ten minutes, reducing the chutney until it is thick.

Remove the solid coconut cream from its clear sachet and cut into small pieces. Add this to the chutney and stir, simmering until it has dissolved completely. Continue to simmer on a very low heat for a further thirty minutes to disperse the coconut flavour (stirring every five minutes at this stage to avoid sticking). Pour into hot, sterilized jars and seal with sterile lids.

Butternut, Apricot and Almond Chutney

Yet another from the fertile mind and active kitchen of Mary Hart!

800g/1lb12oz butternut squash, peeled and
the flesh diced into 1.5cm/½in cubes
400g/15oz white sugar
600ml/1pt malt vinegar
2 large onions, peeled and chopped
225g/8oz soft dried apricots, chopped

½ teaspoon turmeric
15g/¼oz coriander seeds, crushed
15g/¼oz salt
Rind and juice of 1 lemon
Rind and juice of 1 orange
115g/4oz flaked almonds

Place the sugar and vinegar into a pan and heat sufficiently to dissolve the sugar. Add all the other ingredients (excepting the almonds). Bring slowly to the boil, stirring occasionally. Reduce the heat and simmer gently until thick, stirring to prevent sticking to the bottom of the pan. Now add the almond flakes.

Stir well before bottling into sterile jars, sealing and labelling.

Clod Hall Chutney

Carola Morrison runs a very successful B & B at Clod Hall, Milson, Cleobury Mortimer, Shropshire, and included this recipe in a Recipe Calendar compiled and produced on

Butternut, Apricot and Almond Chutney.

behalf of the South Shropshire Farm Holiday Group. She was kind enough to also allow us to use it here. Carola says that 'chutney can be added to stews for extra piquancy'.

1.35kg/3lb cooking apples, peeled, cored and chopped
2 large onions, peeled and chopped
850ml/1½pt malt vinegar
900g/2lb brown sugar
450g/1lb chopped raisins

225g/8oz crystallized ginger, chopped
2 tablespoons turmeric
1 teaspoon salt
2 teaspoons dry mustard
½ teaspoon cayenne pepper

Place the apples and onions in a large pan. Add the vinegar, boil to a pulp. Add the other ingredients and mix in well. Boil again for a further half hour, stirring often.

Ladle into jars and cover.

Apple and Tomato Chutney

Cooking apples make the best chutneys, but, if you have a load of windfall eaters that will not keep, it is possible to use them in almost any recipe that has apples in the list of ingredients. Remember that eating/dessert apples will, however, be sweeter and it might be worth considering reducing your sugar quantities in order to compensate.

2kg/4lb 6oz red tomatoes, peeled and sliced
2kg/4lb 6oz apples
4 onions, peeled and sliced
1.2ltr/2pt white wine vinegar

1 dessertspoon peppercorns
1 tablespoon ground ginger
450g/1lb brown sugar
30g/1oz salt

Put the tomatoes and onions into a large bowl, pour the vinegar over them and add the peppercorns, ginger, salt and sugar before leaving overnight.

Peel, core and slice the apples and put them, along with the previously prepared mixture, into a preserving pan placed over heat. Stir frequently until boiling and then simmer until thick and pulpy (this might take an hour or more).

Spoon into sterilized jars and cover when cold.

Onion and Cherry Tomato Chutney

Although one can never grow enough onions, there are, however, only so many cherry tomatoes one can eat during the summer. Normally, our surpluses get frozen and made into tomato soup during the winter months. As a result of visiting Mary Hart and being given the opportunity to sample the finished product, they might very well be used to make this superb-tasting chutney in the future.

1kg/2lb 3oz cherry tomatoes
1kg/2lb 3oz onions, peeled and finely sliced
4 garlic cloves, peeled and crushed
2 red bird's eye chillies, deseeded and finely chopped

400ml/13fl oz cider vinegar
250g/9oz white sugar
1 tablespoon celery seed
lots of chopped fresh basil

Onion and Cherry Tomato Chutney.

Put the onions, garlic and chilli into a preserving pan together with the vinegar. Bring up to the boil, then simmer until the onions are tender and there is very little liquid left.

Now add the sugar and cherry tomatoes; boil for a short time, then simmer gently until the mixture becomes thick (this could take an hour or more, but it is important not to hurry the process). Remove from the heat and stir in the basil and celery seed.

Spoon the mixture into warm sterile jars; cover and label.

NB: TV cook and author Nigel Slater says that when it comes to adding fresh herbs to any recipe, add as much, or as little, as you like. As Mary Hart obviously likes lots of fresh basil in this particular recipe (and, having tasted the end product, so do we), it is, in the end, all down to a matter of personal taste when it comes to including such ingredients.

Red Tomato Chutney

It is often possible to find locally grown tomatoes at farmers' markets, sometimes by the tray-load and quite cheaply during late summer when there is a glut. As well as using them fresh in cooking and as the main ingredient in soups, which can then be frozen, they produce superb chutney, which can be used as an accompaniment to all manner of meals. This traditional recipe has been given an additional 'twist' by using a *bouquet garni*, rather than relying entirely on shop-bought pickling spices.

1kg/2lb 3oz ripe tomatoes, skinned and
    roughly chopped
2 onions, peeled and finely chopped
1 cooking apple, peeled, cored and finely
    chopped

175g/6oz seedless raisins
2 cloves garlic, peeled and crushed
14g/½oz fresh ginger, scraped and crushed
55g/2oz brown sugar
300ml/10fl oz vinegar

bouquet garni made up of:

1 crushed bay leaf
4–5 cloves
2–3 crushed dried chillies

½ teaspoon mustard seeds
plus a few each of cardamoms, cinnamon,
    coriander and peppercorns

Simmer the chopped onions in a large saucepan with a little water before adding the apple and raisins and cooking gently until they soften. Add the tomatoes, garlic, ginger and sugar and mix together thoroughly before including the vinegar and *bouquet garni*.

Cook on a low heat for about an hour, or until the mixture has thickened so much that when a groove is made across the surface in the pan with a wooden spoon the impression lasts for a few seconds and does not fill up with liquid.

Finally, spoon into hot, clean jars and seal immediately.

Spiced Tomato Chutney

Add a bit of extra 'oomph' to tomato chutney by following this particular recipe from Mary Hart.

1.5kg/3lb 5oz firm, ripe tomatoes, chopped
450g/1lb cooking apples, peeled, cored
    and chopped
1 head of celery, diced
450g/1lb red onions, peeled and chopped
    small
1 hot chilli, deseeded and chopped
675g/1lb 8oz demerara sugar
1 teaspoon coriander seeds, crushed

1 large piece root ginger, scraped and crushed
150ml/5fl oz water
600ml/1pt malt vinegar
4 tablespoons balsamic vinegar
300g/12oz sultanas
1 tablespoon tamarind paste
1 teaspoon salt

Place the tomatoes, apples, celery, onions, chilli and sugar into a preserving pan. Tie the coriander and ginger tightly in a piece of muslin and add to the pan together with the water. Heat gently, stirring until the apples and tomatoes have softened and the onion is tender.

Add both the balsamic and malt vinegars, and the sultanas, tamarind paste and salt, before bringing to the boil, then simmering until thick.

Remember to discard the muslin bag containing the coriander and ginger root before potting up into sterile jars and storing once completely cooled.

Spiced Tomato Chutney.

Runner Bean Chutney

Some household members love runner beans – others hate them. Whichever, they are well worth growing. However, no matter how few plants you grow, there always seems to be so many to harvest that even the keenest runner bean fans tend to begin freezing them long before the season ends. You could, of course, give some away to friends and neighbours, but even they eventually start hiding whenever they see you coming armed with the latest picking! They might be more appreciative of a jar or two of Runner Bean Chutney and it certainly is a more interesting alternative than discovering bags of forgotten beans at the bottom of the freezer in twelve months' time.

750g/1½kg runner beans, chopped or
   sliced
450g/1lb onions, peeled and roughly
   chopped
850ml/1½pt white wine vinegar

450g/1lb demerara sugar
1½ tablespoons each of cornflour, turmeric and
   mustard powder
a little salt

Cook the beans and onions in salted water. Strain off the water and either chop further the beans and onions, or mince them to your favoured texture. Put them and approximately two-thirds of the vinegar back in the pan and heat until simmering.

Add the sugar and heat until it has dissolved. Test for sweetness and, if necessary, add a little more. Mix the cornflour, turmeric and mustard powder with the remainder of the vinegar and stir it into the pan contents until they begin to thicken.

Chopping and preparing runner beans.

Adding sugar to Runner Bean Chutney.

Bottling Runner Bean Chutney.

Simmer for a further twenty minutes and, remembering that this is a sweet chutney, taste again and add more sugar (or turmeric and/or mustard) if required. Heat again until the mixture is at the correct consistency, that is, if you draw a wooden spoon across the bottom of the pan, the chutney remains divided and there is no surplus liquid. Bottle immediately.

NB: Unlike several chutneys, Runner Bean Chutney can be eaten straight away.

Carrot Chutney

Carrots appear in several pickling recipes, but not often as the main ingredient of cooked chutney. In fact, all in all, this Mary Hart recipe has some very interesting ingredients indeed.

900g/2lb carrots, peeled	15g/½oz yellow mustard seeds
150g/5½oz fresh ginger, peeled	500ml/18fl oz cider vinegar
finely grated rind and juice of 2 large lemons	300ml/10fl oz water
1 mild red chilli, deseeded	650g/1lb 8oz white sugar
175g/6oz golden sultanas	125g/4½oz clear honey
30g/1oz salt	1 red and 1 yellow pepper, diced
15g/½oz ground coriander	

Using a mandolin slicer, make strings of the carrots as long as possible. Cut half of the ginger into very fine strips and place the second half into a small electric grinder together with the chilli and a little of the lemon juice. Process until fine.

Combine the carrot, ginger and chilli mix, lemon rind, sultanas, the remainder of the lemon juice, salt, coriander and mustard seed with the vinegar in a bowl. Cover and leave to soak for twelve hours.

Now place in a preserving pan with the water, bring to the boil and simmer for twenty-five minutes before adding the sugar, honey and peppers. Bring back to the boil and simmer until thick. Pot and cover when cold; label and store for three months.

Spicy Ratatouille Chutney

Ann Lambert of Redford, West Sussex, is well known and respected amongst fellow chutney makers; she says that this recipe should make about four 450g/1lb jars and will take about forty-five minutes to prepare plus two to three hours of cooking time. Ann also suggests that 'this is a very hot and spicy chutney – as the name implies. It may be "tamed" a little by using less cayenne pepper and paprika if you wish.'

Spicy Ratatouille Chutney.

500g/1lb 2oz courgettes, thinly sliced
500g/1lb 2oz onions, peeled and chopped
2 peppers – ideally one red and one green
1 medium-sized aubergine, finely chopped
1kg/2lb 3oz tomatoes – good and ripe,
   skinned and chopped

2 good cloves of garlic or 3 smaller ones,
   peeled and crushed
1 tablespoon each of salt, paprika, ground
   coriander and cayenne pepper
1 large cooking apple
300ml/10fl oz malt vinegar
375g/13oz demerara sugar

Put into a large pan the following ingredients: courgettes, onions, peppers, aubergine, tomatoes, garlic, apple, salt, paprika, coriander and cayenne pepper. Cook gently in a covered pan, stirring occasionally until the juices run.

Now boil the mixture very briefly before simmering in the mixture's own juices for one to one and a half hours. Stop when all the vegetables are soft, but their shapes can still be seen. Add the vinegar and sugar. Stir to dissolve this and then cook gently for another hour or so. There should be no vinegar floating on the mixture and the chutney will become quite thick.

Spoon into prepared jars. Cool, label with the name and date and . . . the difficult bit . . . wait for at least two months for it to mature!

Sweet Beetroot Chutney

Another of Mary Hart's recipes – she says it goes well with either cheese or a curry!

900g/1lb15oz raw beetroot, peeled and finely chopped	450g/1lb demerara sugar
	225g/8oz raisins
225g/8oz onions, peeled and finely chopped	1 clove garlic, peeled and crushed
450g/1lb cooking apples, peeled, cored and chopped	salt, to taste
	1 piece root ginger, approximately 7cm/2½in in length, scraped and chopped
rind and juice of 2 large oranges	
850ml/1½pt malt vinegar	10g/¼oz mustard seeds
300ml/10fl oz water	2 star anis (in a muslin bag)

Place the beetroot, onions, apples, orange rind and juice in a preserving pan before adding the vinegar and water. Bring to the boil: reduce the heat and simmer until the beetroot is tender.

Add the sugar, raisins, garlic, salt, ginger, mustard seeds and star anis. Simmer gently, stirring until the mixture is thick.

Remove the muslin bag containing the star anis and bottle into warm sterilized jars before covering, sealing, labelling and storing once cold.

Red Cabbage and Apple Chutney

Philip and his wife Tricia were at a village fête in West Sussex when they met up with this chutney and its originator, Samantha Coley. She was kind enough to give us permission to include it here and says it is 'fantastic with cheese and cold meat'.

500g/1lb 2oz red cabbage, finely sliced – but do not use the hard centre	2 teaspoons smoked paprika
	2 teaspoons ground turmeric
300g/10½oz cooking apples, cubed (still with the skin on)	1 cinnamon stick
	250g/9oz brown sugar
2 tablespoons finely chopped fresh ginger	400ml/13fl oz white wine vinegar

Put all the ingredients together in a large heavy-based pan and bring the mixture to the boil. Reduce the heat as low as possible and simmer for four hours; stir every quarter of an hour or so, or until the chutney thickens. Remove the cinnamon stick.

Transfer to warm, dry jars and put on airtight lids. Leave to mature in a cool, dark place for about a month before using.

Fiery Marrow and Courgette Chutney

There are those who say that marrows are fit for nothing and certainly of no value to the chutney and pickle maker, but, in fact, mature marrows are excellent for wine or jam making, or pickle and chutney production. Ideally, one should remove the fruits of courgettes and marrows when quite small; courgettes at about 10cm/4in in length, marrows approximately twice that size. They do, however, seem to grow overnight without one ever noticing, until suddenly you are faced with an overlarge 'fruit' that one really doesn't know what to do with. Guess what? We do!

Red Cabbage and Apple Chutney.

1kg/2lb 3oz marrow, peeled and diced
1kg/2lb 3oz courgettes, diced
55g/2oz salt
250g/9oz onions, peeled and diced
15g/½oz mustard seeds
15g/½oz turmeric
8g/¼oz cayenne pepper
8g/¼oz ground ginger
1ltr/1¾pt white malt vinegar
500g/1lb 2oz white sugar

For a spice bag
50g/1¾oz fresh ginger, diced
12 whole cloves
10 black peppercorns
2 bay leaves, broken

Put the diced marrow and courgette into a bowl, sprinkle with the salt and leave overnight to 'strew'. Next day, drain off the liquid and rinse off any residual salt – allow it to drain or pat it dry with kitchen roll.

Place the marrow and courgette into a pan, together with the onions, turmeric, cayenne pepper, mustard seeds, ground ginger, vinegar and the spice bag. Bring slowly to the boil before adding the sugar (stirring all the time). Reduce the heat and cook gently until thick. Remove the spice bag before bottling in the usual way.

Marrow and Apple Chutney

What do you do when someone gives you a huge marrow and a bag of cooking apples from the orchard? Make this delicious Marrow and Apple Chutney from Mary Hart's recipe book, that's what!

900g/2lb marrow, peeled and diced
3 teaspoons salt (for preparing marrow)
900g/2lb cooking apples, peeled, cored and
    chopped
400g/14oz white onions, peeled and chopped
1ltr/1¾pt white malt vinegar
550g/1lb 4oz white sugar

2 teaspoons yellow mustard seeds
30g/1oz fresh ginger, peeled crushed and
    placed in a muslin bag
225g/8oz yellow sultanas
¼ teaspoon cayenne pepper
½ teaspoon turmeric

Remove the peel and seeds from the marrow and cut into small, dice-shaped pieces before placing them in a bowl and sprinkling with salt. Leave overnight, and the next day, drain off the liquid before placing the marrow into a preserving pan together with the chopped apples and onions.

Now add the vinegar, sugar, mustard seeds and ginger (having secured it tightly in a muslin bag). Bring to the boil stirring, then simmer until everything is softened. Now add the sultanas, cayenne pepper and turmeric.

Simmer until the mixture becomes thick, remove the muslin bag of ginger, then pot into warm, sterile jars. Allow to mature before using.

Beatrice Laval's Lavender Chutney

This glorious, fragrant chutney has its origins in rural France. Beatrice Laval uses it as an accompaniment to French cheese, with which it 'marries' very well.

20 lavender flowers, chopped into small
    pieces
3 lemons, washed and roughly chopped
white wine vinegar (enough to cover the
    chopped lemons)
3 onions, peeled and finely chopped

85g/3oz sultanas
2 tablespoons mustard seeds
1 cinnamon stick
pinch ground allspice
salt to taste
sugar to taste

Remove the pips and pith from the lemons and, in a bowl, cover them with vinegar before leaving to stand overnight.

Place the lemons and vinegar into a pan and add the remainder of the ingredients. Stir until the sugar has dissolved, then bring the pan's contents to the boil before reducing the heat and simmering gently until the mixture thickens.

Remove the cinnamon stick before spooning or pouring into warmed storage jars and sealing tightly.

Onion Marmalade Chutney

Onion Marmalade or Onion Marmalade Chutney seems to be very popular at the moment and is regularly served at the end of a restaurant meal along with cheese and biscuits. This is how Laurence Murphy of *Fat Olives*, Emsworth, Hampshire makes his.

6 onions, peeled and sliced
30g/1oz butter
1 medium glass white wine
1 bay leaf
8 black peppercorns

4 dessertspoons honey
small bunch of thyme bound together with string
115g/4oz castor sugar
6 dessertspoons white wine vinegar
salt and pepper to season

Sweat the onions in the butter before adding the white wine and reducing until it has nearly disappeared. Add the other ingredients and reduce over a low heat until it begins to thicken. Taste (if it is too sweet, add more vinegar) and season.

Allow to cool before placing in a sterilized jar and storing in a suitably cool place.

Uncooked Green Tomato Chutney

And then there are, of course, some chutneys that do not need to be cooked at all! This is based on an old Sussex recipe.

Onion Marmalade Chutney served with pigeon breast.

Uncooked Green Tomato Chutney.

450g/1lb green tomatoes	500ml/18fl oz malt vinegar
450g/1lb stoneless dates	1 teaspoon salt
450g/1lb cooking apples, peeled and cored	¼ teaspoon ground white pepper
450g/1lb onions, peeled	¼ teaspoon cayenne pepper
450g/1lb sultanas	15g/½oz fresh ginger, peeled and minced
450g/1lb brown sugar	10g/¼oz pickling spice (in a muslin bag)

Chop the first five ingredients in a food processor, then place in a stainless steel bowl with the sugar, vinegar, salt, peppers, ginger and spice bag. Stir and mix occasionally for twenty-four hours, keeping the bowl covered in between stirring. After this time, remove the spice bag and bottle into sterile jars. Enjoy now or later – it is reckoned to keep for up to three years!

NB: Be careful not to 'overdose' any recipes containing pepper, especially black pepper, as too much will obviously influence all the other flavours.

Apricot Chutney

Choose ripe, mature fruit of ideal quality for eating fresh or cooking. They should not be mushy, but they also should not be rock hard: just as ripe as you would eat them fresh. Apricot chutney goes well with lamb (especially lamb shanks) and chicken – or so thought Molly Harris, who gave me the basics of this recipe a long time ago. (Long-time devotees to *The Archers* on BBC Radio 4 may well remember Molly as Martha Woodforde, the kind-hearted village gossip.)

1.5kg/3lb 5oz fresh apricots, stoned and chopped	600ml/1pt cider vinegar
	225g/8oz demerara sugar
350g/12oz onions, peeled and finely chopped	1 dessertspoon salt
	1 dessertspoon mustard seeds
2 cloves garlic, peeled and crushed	1 teaspoon each of ground cinnamon and mace
small piece fresh ginger, cleaned and grated	½ teaspoon ground cayenne pepper

Simplicity itself! Place all the ingredients into a preserving pan and simmer gently until the ingredients meld and become soft and thick.

Spoon into sterilized jars and seal.

Red Onion and Courgette Chutney

Ann Brockhurst of Fernhurst, Haslemere, Surrey knows a great deal about making jams, chutneys and pickles. She very kindly submitted this particular recipe, for which we are very grateful.

Red Onion and Courgette Chutney.

Clear and attractive labelling enhances any jar of chutney or pickle.

1kg/2lb 3oz courgettes, peeled and diced
4 large red onions, peeled and diced
1 tablespoon coriander seeds
125g/4½oz fresh ginger
2 teaspoons black mustard seeds

500ml/18fl oz cider vinegar
200g/7oz sultanas or raisins
1 tablespoon salt
350g/12oz white granulated sugar

Whiz the diced courgettes and onions with the coriander seeds and fresh ginger in a food processor or grinder. Leave the mustard seeds whole. Bring all the ingredients together, excepting for the sugar and salt, and then simmer for fifteen minutes.

Now add the sugar and salt and simmer until most of the liquid has evaporated and you are happy with the consistency.

Bottle as normal and allow to mature.

Stephan Langton Chutney

The Stephan Langton, Friday Street, is set in a tranquil valley on the privately owned Wooton Estate, just a few miles west of Dorking in the heart of the Surrey Hills Area of Outstanding Natural Beauty. Chef Simon Adams loves to create new dishes using fresh local produce and whatever is in season. Classics include homemade Pork Pie and Picca-lilli and a Ploughman's dish using local cheeses served with delicious homemade bread and Stephan Langton Chutney. Rosie Robinson tells us that although it is basically an

A selection of produce from Stonham Hedgerow.

Recipes for Characterful Chutneys

The chef at The Stephan Langton at Friday Street, Surrey adapts his basic chutney ingredients according to the season.

apple chutney, 'We adapt it according to the season we are in, for example the last batch was plum and apple; we have also had pear and apple and green tomato and apple. And when there is no glut of fruit, we just go back to the basic recipe.'

6 large cooking apples, peeled, cored and cut into bite-size chunks
200g/7oz tomatoes, peeled and deseeded
1 onion, peeled and chopped
50g/1¾oz each of raisins and sultanas
1 orange, zest and juice
1 pineapple, peeled and with the core and top removed

250g/9oz granulated sugar
2 teaspoons salt
½ teaspoon each of cinnamon, ground nutmeg, ground ginger, and cayenne pepper
small pinch of saffron threads
250ml/8fl oz white wine vinegar

Put all the ingredients in a heavy-bottomed saucepan. Place on a low heat and stir frequently to avoid the mixture sticking. The chutney takes about one and a half hours of very gentle cooking before it starts to look like jam. Use a wooden spoon to scrape the bottom of the pan and if the mixture has no juices running in the path of the spoon, it is done.

Put in a jar and leave to cool completely before sealing it. Store in the fridge or cellar.

Recipes for Pickles and Pickling

The basic difference between a chutney and a pickle is usually described by those in the know as being that chutneys are cooked for a long time and set in the jar, whilst true pickles are either raw or just par-boiled and the preserving agent is mainly vinegar with a little salt. There is, however, quite a crossover of names, especially when it comes to describing sweet pickles, normally made from fruits or sweeter-tasting vegetables that are cooked slowly in a syrup of vinegar and sugar: spiced pineapple pickle and several others featured here are made by incorporating basic chutney-making methods – and yet they are called 'pickles'! So we thought we'd start this particular section with some of the more ambiguously named before passing on to more clearly defined *pickling* recipes containing ingredients that are pickled cold and raw, or maybe just slightly cooked.

Pepper Pot Pickle

Is it a pickle, is it a chutney? Whichever, it tastes very good and we are once again most grateful to Mary Hart for her generosity in allowing us to use her recipe.

450g/1lb cooking apples, peeled and
    chopped
450g/1lb onions, peeled and chopped
4 garlic cloves, peeled and crushed
900g/1lb15oz mixture of red, green and
    yellow Bell peppers, deseeded and diced
4 medium-hot chillies (Serrano or similar),
    deseeded and chopped

450g/1lb demerara sugar
2 teaspoons Tabasco sauce
300ml/10fl oz red wine vinegar
85ml/2½fl oz balsamic vinegar
1 tablespoon tamarind paste
2 large carrots, scraped and finely diced

Place the apples, onions, garlic, tamarind paste, peppers and chillies into a preserving pan, together with the sugar and Tabasco sauce. Simmer very carefully over a low heat (bearing in mind the fact that there is at this stage very little liquid included and it is easy to burn). Stir frequently until the apples, onions, peppers and chillies have all become soft. Add the vinegars and carrots and cook slowly until thick.
    Place in warmed, sterile jars; seal and label.

Pepper Pot Pickle.

Spiced Pineapple Pickle

Andrew and Jacquie Pern, owners of *The Star Inn*, Harome, Helmsley, North Yorkshire very kindly (particularly as Andrew has published a recipe book of his own, *Black Pudding and Foie Gras* (May 2008)), allowed us to include this rich, golden chutney, which they use in their restaurant.

1 pineapple, skinned, cored and finely chopped
1 clove garlic, peeled and crushed
1 teaspoon grain mustard
3 tablespoons white wine vinegar

pinch saffron strands
150g/5oz demerara sugar
pinch of salt

Place all the ingredients into a heavy-bottomed pan; stir in a pinch of salt and simmer gently for about one and a half hours, until a golden yellow colour.

When at the right consistency, spoon into an airtight jar. Leave to cool before sealing the jar. This can be made in advance and will keep for three to four weeks.

Pineapple Chilli Pickle

Unlike the Spiced Pineapple Pickle above, this particular recipe needs at least two month's storage to be at its best.

Pineapple Chilli Pickle.

1kg/2lb 3oz pineapple, peeled and finely chopped
3 large onions, peeled and finely chopped
375g/13oz light brown sugar
300ml/10fl oz white wine vinegar
3 finger chillies, deseeded and very finely chopped

6 teaspoons Madras curry powder
1½ teaspoons ground ginger
1½ teaspoons salt
1½ teaspoons celery seeds

Place all the ingredients into a preserving pan and heat gently, stirring frequently. Cook slowly until the mixture thickens to the right consistency prior to bottling.

Mildly Spicy Melon Pickle

Use cantaloupe, Charente or honeydew melons for this recipe. A variation of this pickle is commonly served in and around the region where Jeremy lives in France – just north of the huge melon-growing area between Thouars and Loudun. The Haut-Poitou area is France's third largest melon-producing region, and those sold under the label *Les Maîtres du melon du Haut-Poitou* account for some 15 per cent of overall production. The pickle goes well with the smoked and cured cold meats that are also readily found in the same part of France.

3 × 1kg/2lb 3oz (approx.) melons
water, for blanching
300ml/10fl oz white wine vinegar
450g/1lb white sugar
1 lemon, sliced

4 cloves
1 cinnamon stick
1 dried red chilli
1 teaspoon allspice (either in a sachet or tied
    in a muslin bag)

Remove the skin and seeds from the melons and cube the flesh. Boil a large pan of water and in it blanch the melon cubes for between one to two minutes before draining and refreshing in cold (iced) water. Drain again and pat dry with either a clean tea towel or kitchen roll, before gently packing the softened melon pieces in sterilized preserving jars – wide-necked jars will help facilitate this.

In a pan, and stirring all the time, heat the vinegar, sugar, lemon and spices until all the sugar has dissolved. Boil and then simmer for a further twenty minutes. Remove the lemon slices, cinnamon stick and allspice before carefully pouring the liquid into the jars and over the melon cubes. Secure the lids whilst still hot and leave for a month to mature and infuse.

Elderberry Pickle

Apart from perhaps blackberries, there can be nothing more traditional and best suited to a book that includes ingredients gathered from the hedgerow than elderberries. As

Elderberries can be quite versatile and used in chutneys, jams and wines – and what's more, they're free!

with the majority of pickles and chutneys, this particular recipe tastes better if you allow it to mature for a few weeks before eating it.

450g/1lb elderberries
1.3kg/2lb 12oz apples
100g/3½oz stoned prunes
55g/2oz sultanas
55g/2oz stem ginger

850ml/1½pt white wine vinegar
550g/1lb 3oz dark brown sugar
2 teaspoons ground allspice
90ml/3fl oz ginger wine

Remove the elderberries from their stems, wash them lightly and dry well. Peel and core the apples and chop them into medium chunks. Chop the prunes into small chunks. Place all the ingredients into a large heavy-bottomed pan and cook until the sugar has dissolved. Bring the mixture to the boil, then simmer for an hour, stirring occasionally, until it has thickened.

Have some warm, well-cleaned jam jars waiting and pour or ladle the mixture into them. Seal at once with well fitting screw tops.

Apple, Onion and Mint Pickle

Way back in the 1970s, Yorkshire Television ran a very successful series called *Farmhouse Kitchen*, which was hosted by Dorothy Sleightholme. As a spin-off from the series, Trident Television produced several recipe books, one of which was *Farmhouse Kitchen II*, published in 1978. Still available through secondhand book shops, it contains many interesting recipes, of which this is one. It was submitted by Stella Boldy of Sykehouse, North Humberside.

450g/1lb hard cooking apples
225g/8oz onions
2 teaspoons lemon juice
3–4 tablespoons fresh mint leaves, finely chopped
75g/3½oz castor sugar

2 teaspoons mustard
½ level teaspoon ground ginger
2 level teaspoons salt
200ml/7fl oz white, or cider vinegar

Peel and mince the apples and onions and add the lemon juice before mixing in the chopped mint leaves. In a pan, dissolve the sugar, mustard, ground ginger and salt in a little of the vinegar and simmer for ten minutes.

In a separate pan, bring the remainder of the vinegar to boil and pour it over the sugar/spice mixture. Allow to go cold before mixing the liquid into the apples, onions and mint. Put into clean jars with vinegar-proof lids.

NB: Stella Boldy claimed that the pickle should be stored for a month and can be kept for up to three months.

An apple harvest ripe for inclusion in Apple, Onion and Mint Pickle.

Plum, Pear and Carrot Pickle

When we were given this recipe by Mary Hart, she had, in fact, called it a chutney rather than a pickle (and we beg her forgiveness for changing its definition). The main reason for changing its name and placing it in this particular section of the book is due to the fact that having tasted it, it is the nearest thing to Branston Pickle that you can get without it actually *being* Branston Pickle. Mind you, for the advertisers, 'Bring out the Plum, Pear and Carrot Pickle ...' doesn't have quite the same snappy ring to it does it? But, there again, once tried, we don't think that there would be any need to advertise this particular recipe!

1kg/2lb 3oz plums, quartered and stoned
750g/1lb10oz pears, peeled, cored and diced
750g/1lb10oz cooking apples, peeled, cored and diced
500g/1lb 2oz shallots, peeled and diced
500g/1lb 2oz carrots, peeled and diced
250g/9oz prunes, stoned and chopped
500g/1lb 2oz soft brown sugar
600ml/1pt cider vinegar

For the spice bag
55g/2oz root ginger, scraped and diced
1 hot chilli, deseeded and chopped
2 teaspoons mustard seeds
3 teaspoons black peppercorns

Place the spices in a muslin square and tie it tightly. Place this and all the ingredients (excepting the carrots) into a large pan and bring to the boil slowly, stirring occasionally.

Simmer the mixture for about one and a half hours, then add the carrots before continuing to cook until the mixture is thick.

Pot into warm, sterile jars, pack down well in order to remove any air bubbles, then seal and label.

Microwave Mango Pickle

The preparation of pickles (and chutneys) is usually based on traditional methods and utensils. There is, however, no reason why, provided that a few important principles are adhered to, some recipes should not be done in a microwave. The quantities given here should fill one 450g/1lb jar.

3 mangoes, peeled and cut into small pieces
2.5cm/1in piece fresh root ginger, finely chopped
1 small green chilli, deseeded and finely chopped
115g/4oz soft light brown sugar

200ml/7fl oz cider vinegar
½ level teaspoon ground ginger
1 garlic clove, peeled and crushed

Place all the ingredients into a large bowl and microwave on 'high' for five minutes, or until the sugar has dissolved. Stir occasionally. Three-quarters cover the bowl with cling film and further microwave on 'high' for another twenty minutes, or until thick and well reduced (stir two or three times during cooking and after every minute for the last five minutes in order to prevent the surface of the chutney from drying out. Allow to stand for five minutes before spooning into sterilized jars in the usual fashion. Cover and store for three months.

Worcester Plum Pickle

Writing a book of this nature is a delight, not only because of the recipes learnt and used, but also because of the enthusiastic people we get to meet. Sally Hallstead offered the following recipe, which apparently was frequently made by her mother-in-law. Sally says that this particular pickle is 'just right for eating with any cold meat, but I remember it best when it was used by my mother-in-law alongside one of her own, very special cold game pies which she made after my father-in-law's various shooting expeditions'.

450g/1lb plums, washed, dried and destalked
225g/8oz sugar
300ml/10fl oz white vinegar
rind of half a lemon

small piece fresh root ginger, bruised
4 whole cloves
1 cinnamon stick

Prick the plums all over with a fork before placing them in a pan. Add the vinegar and sugar. Make a *bouquet garni* of the lemon rind and spices by tying them tightly into a small square of muslin and add this to the pan also. Heat gently, stirring all the time until the plums are tender (but do not leave them so long that the skins split).

Gently remove the plums from the liquid mixture with a perforated spoon and place into storage jars. Remove the *bouquet garni* before boiling the liquid rapidly for five minutes more. Pour over the plums and immediately seal the jars. For the best-tasting pickled Worcester plums, store in a cool, dark place for at least a month before using.

Military Pickle

Mike Davies has run the extremely successful Damerham Fisheries near Fordingbridge, Hampshire for many years and has quite a reputation as being a highly skilled business-man, fly fisher and bar-room raconteur. Mike says, 'I cannot claim to have invented it: I found it printed in an old book and can only assume some old buffer brought it back from India to combat malaria, but found that a gin and tonic worked better!'

1 marrow
1 cauliflower
450g/1lb green beans
salt, sufficient to cover chopped marrow,
    cauliflower and green beans
450g/1lb onions, peeled and chopped
450g/1lb demerara sugar

2.3ltr/4pt wine or cider vinegar
7 chillies, deseeded and chopped
30g/1oz turmeric powder
30g/1oz ground ginger
115g/4oz plain flour
cold water (to make paste of the dry
    ingredients)

Cut the marrow, cauliflower and green beans into small pieces and cover with the salt. Leave to stand overnight, then drain. Put into a large saucepan and add the sugar, vinegar, and chillies, then boil together for five minutes.

Mix together the remaining dry ingredients into a paste with a little cold water, then add to the pan. Boil for thirty minutes, stirring all the time in order to prevent the contents burning on contact with the bottom of the pan.

Let it cool, bottle it and enjoy!

Golden Glory Peach Pickle

This Indian-style sweet pickle is an excellent accompaniment to some curry dishes and is also good with cheese and crackers. Appropriately enough, Hall & Woodhouse, Dorset brewers, have a premium ale called Golden Glory, which has a subtle aroma of peach and melon and would, we imagine, be a great drink to go with a curry and/or peach pickle.

2kg/4lb 6oz peaches, peeled and sliced
175g/6oz raisins
115g/4oz onion, peeled and chopped
150g/5½oz preserved ginger, chopped
2 cloves garlic, peeled and crushed
1.5kg/3½lb brown sugar

1.2ltr/2pt cider vinegar
55g/2oz pickling or allspice (or equivalent in
    sachets)
1½ tablespoons chilli powder
1 tablespoon mustard seed
1 teaspoon curry powder

In a heavy-bottomed pan, stir together all the ingredients. If using loose spice, wrap it in a small piece of muslin and tie the top together tightly with string. Bring the pan to the boil, then simmer over a medium heat for about one and a half hours, or until the chutney is at the preferred consistency. Stir occasionally during cooking.

Remove the sachets/*bouquet garni* of spices and spoon the mixture into warm, sterilized jars.

Indian Lime Pickle

Garam masala is a mixture of ground spices and is used a lot in Indian cooking. The actual 'recipe' varies according to the regions of India in which it is found. Typically, however, they might include peppercorns, cloves, bay leaves, cumin seeds, cinnamon, cardamom and coriander. Some recipes blend spices with herbs, others with liquids such as vinegar (as here). Commercial blends can be bought ready ground.

4 green limes, quartered
2 teaspoons salt
2.5cm/1in piece root ginger, sliced
2 tablespoons oil
1 tablespoon white vinegar
10 cayenne chillies, deseeded and sliced

1 tablespoon paprika
1 teaspoon garam masala
1 teaspoon cumin seeds
2 garlic cloves, peeled and sliced
2 tablespoons sugar

Lime Pickle.

Place the lime quarters (unpeeled) in a large jar, together with one teaspoon of salt before sealing the jar tightly. Shake the jar to mix thoroughly in the salt and leave in a light or sunny spot for three to four days. Shake the jar regularly. After three to four days, add the other teaspoon of salt, shake and leave for one month in the sun. Rotate the jar every day.

When ready to prepare the pickle, heat the oil in a pan and cook the ginger till golden. Add the vinegar, sugar, limes and lime juice from the jar. Mix well and cook for about five minutes. Add the spices, garlic and chillies and cook for a further three minutes.

Store in sterilized jars and keep in the fridge for up to one month.

Tindora Pickle

Tindora is a type of gherkin, the 'fruits' of which may be eaten either when green and immature, or red and ripe. Pickle masala (an ingredient of this recipe) can either be made, or bought as Pickle Masala Pickle Mix – a commercially produced blend with which to create any amount of Indian pickle menus.

350g/12oz tindora, washed, dried and chopped
15ml/½fl oz white wine vinegar
15ml/½fl oz extra virgin olive oil

salt to taste
3 tablespoons Pickle Masala Pickle Mix

Place the chopped tindora into a mixing bowl, add the vinegar and salt and mix together well. Cover with cling-film and set aside for a couple of hours. Add the pickle mix, making sure that each piece of tindora is well coated.

Add the oil and mix again before bottling and storing (Tindora Pickle will keep in a fridge for about a week).

Chow-Chow

Not, in this particular instance, a breed of dog, Chow-Chow Pickle is perhaps better known in the United States than it is in Britain. The word 'Chou' means edible in Chinese and it is possible that this pickle got its name through an Anglicization. This recipe is, in fact, adapted from an American series of publications called *The Gourmet Cook Book*, the first of which was published in 1950.

450g/1lb small courgettes, chopped and diced
450g/1lb cucumbers, chopped and diced
450g/1lb shallots, peeled
450g/1lb green tomatoes, quartered
450g/1lb French or runner beans, stringed and
   chopped
450g/1lb celery stalks, chopped
450g/1lb cauliflower florets

6 red peppers, deseeded and chopped
450g/1lb onions, peeled and chopped
1.5ltr/2½pt cider vinegar
4 tablespoons flour
225g/8oz sugar
3 tablespoons dry mustard powder
1 teaspoon turmeric

Place all the prepared vegetable ingredients into a large bowl and cover with a brining solution made up of 115g/4oz of salt to 1.2ltr/2pt water and let them stand overnight.

Drain and rinse with fresh water. Allow to dry. Transfer the vegetables into a preserving pan and add the cider vinegar; bring slowly to the boil. Mix together the flour, sugar, mustard powder and turmeric and, using a little extra vinegar, bind together until you have a smooth paste. Stir this paste into the boiling vegetables and simmer for five minutes, stirring constantly.

Fill warm sterile jars to almost overflowing and seal at once.

Marrow Pickle

When I left home at the age of sixteen, my mother gave me a small recipe book produced by Belling, the manufacturer of ovens. I guess that it would have been given away with new cookers and it is nowadays very tatty, has several pages missing and is at least sixty years old. Nevertheless, it has some good, tried and tested recipes (the one for scones has never failed me!) and this basic marrow pickle recipe is as good a way as any of using up a marrow.

1kg/2lb 3oz marrow (after peeling)	10g/¼oz curry powder
115g/4oz salt	6 peppercorns
115g/4oz sugar	500ml/18fl oz malt vinegar
2 level teaspoons ground ginger	20g/¾oz mustard

Marrow Pickle with Camembert – perfect for a picnic!

Cut up the marrow, sprinkle with salt and allow it to stand overnight. Drain off the excess moisture.

Add all the other ingredients to the vinegar; boil for five minutes, then add the drained marrow and cook until tender.

Pack the pickle into jars and seal.

PICKLING THE TRADITIONAL WAY

As we mentioned at the beginning of this chapter, some pickles are more like chutneys in that they are produced by long, slow cooking. Done traditionally though, pickling is the process of preserving food in an acid solution, usually vinegar, but occasionally oils, sometimes aided by brining in salted water – many vegetable pickles are made by brining raw vegetables, draining them and then packing firmly into jars before covering them with spiced vinegar and sealing tightly. It is interesting to relate that many of the 1,000-year-old 'bog bodies' found in Northern Europe have been so well preserved because the peat found in bogs contains an acid that is almost identical in pH levels to the best pickling vinegar!

And then, of course, there is the famous story of how Lord Nelson's body was brought back from the Battle of Trafalgar by the very simple expedient of pickling it in brandy. In fact, Royal Navy chief petty officers are known to celebrate the Battle of Trafalgar by holding an annual 'Pickle Night'. Some say that it is in honour of the ship *HMS Pickle* that fought alongside the *Victory*, but more believe that it is in remembrance of the pickling of Horatio's mortal remains. However, we digress!

Cauliflower Pickle

In Europe, many pickles are made from vegetables. In Turkey, typical ingredients might include cabbage, carrots, beetroot and even turnips; whilst in Greece and Italy pickles are made out of onions, carrots, celery and cauliflower. Mark Twain famously said that 'cauliflower is nothing but cabbage with a college education'. Whether it is or not, it is a pity not to be more imaginative with this popular garden vegetable.

700ml/1¼pt water	½ teaspoon cayenne pepper
225g/8oz cauliflower florets, trimmed and cut into pieces approximately 4cm/1½in long	½ teaspoon turmeric
	1 tablespoon cumin seeds, dry-roasted
fresh ginger root (about 4cm/1½in in length), scraped and thinly sliced	1 teaspoon sea salt
	125ml/4fl oz sesame oil

Boil the water and blanch the cauliflower florets plus the ginger root slices for about one minute. Drain and spread them on a biscuit tray before drying them outdoors in the sunshine, or (bearing in mind British weather!) in a warm oven (95°C/200°F) for about an hour.

Meanwhile, in a mixing bowl, place the cayenne, turmeric, cumin seeds (dry-roast them by placing them briefly in a heated frying pan to which no oil has been added) and salt. Mix together well before adding the cauliflower and ginger slices; toss all together to ensure a thorough coating. Place in a sterilized 500g/1pt Kilner jar or similar.

In a small saucepan, gently heat the sesame oil before pouring it over the cauliflower/ginger mix. Seal with a non-metallic lid and place the jar in a sunny place for a fortnight, giving it a gentle shake several times daily. Store in the usual way after this time, but, once the jar has been opened to use, store it in the fridge from then on.

Red Cabbage Pickle

This traditional pickle is known in almost all of Britain's regions – probably due to its suitability as an accompaniment to cold meats and some hard cheeses.

2 red cabbages	1 tablespoon black peppercorns
85g/3oz salt	1 dessertspoon coriander seeds
600ml/1pt red wine vinegar	small piece fresh ginger
600ml/1pt distilled malt vinegar	4 bay leaves
4 whole dried chillies	1 tablespoon juniper berries

Quarter the cabbages and remove the stem and core. Shred very finely and place in a bowl, sprinkling the layers with salt, and leave for twenty-four hours.

Meanwhile, put the vinegars into a pan and add all the spices, with the exception of the bay leaves and junipers. Bring to the boil, then simmer for five minutes before placing to one side to cool.

Red Cabbage Pickle.

Next day, wash and drain the cabbage and pack into four jars with the bay leaves and juniper berries. Pour in the strained vinegar and tightly seal the lids.

Pickled Christmas Field Mushrooms in Olive Oil

Some years, it is possible to find any amount of field mushrooms out in the wild. In other years they are as rare as the proverbial hen's teeth. If, however, you do happen to hit upon a surfeit one early autumn day, you might like to try suffusing them in good quality olive oil and bringing them out on Christmas Day as an Italian-inspired 'antipasto' to be speared and eaten with a cocktail stick. Get out early in the morning and choose only the freshest and smallest specimens as the larger examples are likely to be more watery, less flavoursome and better used in a traditional breakfast fry-up. And the earlier warning about ensuring you haven't picked a poisonous variety cannot be repeated too often. Assuming that you have a good morning's harvest, the brine quantities given here should be more than sufficient for roughly 1kg/2lb 3oz of mushrooms. You will also need a fair quantity of decent olive oil – exactly how much depends on how many mushrooms you can find!

approx. 1kg/2lb 3oz of field mushrooms

For the brine
500ml/18fl oz white wine vinegar   5 cloves
300ml/10fl oz water   3 bay leaves
1 tablespoon salt

Take great care with the mushrooms: wipe them carefully, but do not wash them as you will only add to their natural water content. Depending on their size, trim or remove their stems, peel the caps if necessary and either slice, halve or quarter each mushroom.

Next, place all the brining ingredients together in a heavy-bottomed pan and bring to the boil. Add the mushroom pieces and further boil for about five minutes.

Drain the mushrooms carefully and spread them out on a baking tray or similar, onto which a spotlessly clean thick tea towel or a good pad of kitchen roll has been laid. Allow to cool and thoroughly dry (it is imperative that the least amount of water is included with the mushrooms once bottled).

Spoon some of the mushrooms into the bottom of previously sterilized preserving jars – the least hand contact you make with them the better, because bacteria on your skin could affect the subsequent keeping quality of the mushrooms. Add a little olive oil and gently agitate to ensure that each of the mushroom pieces is well coated. Add more mushrooms and more oil until each jar is filled to the neck.

Seal tightly and store until Christmas – or for at least a month!

Asparagus in Pickled Onion Juice

Why should cooking of any description be difficult? If you want to cheat in certain aspects … well, why not? Valerie Hardy, a countryside writer and interviewer, tells us that she has made many successful pickles by simply reusing the pickling vinegars and juices left over after finishing a jar of homemade pickled onions. Valerie says she's not sure about the health aspect of doing so, but, as she points out, 'I'm 77, have drunk well water from what subsequently proved to be contaminated when I lived in Wales for ten years, and have always enjoyed a glass or two of gin every evening – I cannot even remember having a cold … I love asparagus … Galen, the ancient physician said that it was cleansing and healing … so what if it makes your urine smell?'

Should you wish to follow Valerie's suggestions, she says asparagus pickles well by such a method as she describes. (By the way, the reason urine smells after eating asparagus is because of a breakdown of beneficial amino acids during digestion!)

450g/1lb asparagus
as much juice as is necessary from previous onion picklings

Boil a large pan of water and plunge the asparagus into it. Cook for two minutes only, so that they are merely blanched. Drain and rinse under cold running water before cutting the asparagus spears sufficiently to stand end-on in clean, sterilized preserving jars. Pour the pickled onion juice into the jars and cover.

Traditionally made Piccalilli such as can be seen here is a far more subtle and attractive colour than that often seen on the supermarket shelf.

Piccalilli (Mustard Pickle)

The vibrant yellow Piccalilli often seen on the shelves of most supermarkets is miles apart from this traditional recipe. Try it and see!

2 cucumbers
450g/1lb onions, peeled
1 small to medium-sized marrow
2 cauliflowers
225g/8oz French beans
30g/1oz salt
1.2ltr/2pt white malt vinegar

30g/1oz pickling spice
225g/8oz demerara sugar
1 rounded dessertspoon ground ginger
1 rounded dessertspoon turmeric
1 rounded dessertspoon mustard
1 rounded dessertspoon flour

Cut the vegetables into small, even pieces, put into a bowl or dish; sprinkle with the salt. Cover and leave for twelve hours, then drain.

Boil two-thirds of the vinegar with the pickling spice for four or five minutes and then strain. Mix the remaining ingredients with the remaining vinegar, return to the pan and bring to the boil. Add the vegetables and mix well. Simmer for ten minutes.

Cool the mixture in the pan, put into jars and cover.

Theo's Pickled Fennel

We met Theo Cartwright at a flower and produce show in Gloucestershire where he had some fine fennel bulbs as part of a five-vegetable entry. He told us that, not only does he use fennel boiled and served with a white sauce, he also pickles it and uses the results in salads. Fennel is sometimes known as Florence fennel or finocchio. The measurements here are apparently sufficient to fill one 450g/1lb jar. Theo also suggests adding a couple of small fennel fronds (the 'leaves') after packing the jars and before adding the preserving liquid.

2 medium-sized fennel bulbs, cut into
    matchstick-thick long strips
1 teaspoon fine sea salt
zest of half an orange
100ml/3½fl oz fresh orange juice

100ml/3½fl oz white wine vinegar
15g/½oz white sugar
4 black peppercorns, lightly cracked in a pestle
    and mortar

Place the fennel strips into a bowl and cover with the sea salt before leaving them to stand for at least an hour. Next, drain any resultant liquid thoroughly and add the zest of half an orange. Fold together well, then pack the mixture into a clean 450g/1lb sterilized jar.

In a heavy-bottomed saucepan heat the remaining ingredients and simmer gently until all the sugar is dissolved – about three minutes.

Carefully pour the liquid over the fennel/orange zest; seal and let it rest for three hours before storing. Unlike some vegetables preserved by pickling, it is recommended that this particular recipe can be used after about a day, but within not more than a month.

Marsh Samphire Pickle

Samphire can be used raw in salads, though it tends to be a little salty, so try boiling or steaming it first. It is very seasonal, growing only in late July/August, and it does not freeze well, so, to be able to use it at any other time, it will be necessary to use traditional pickling methods.

1.4kg/3¼lb wild samphire shoots
12 garlic cloves, peeled and scored
850ml/1½pt water

850ml/1½pt white vinegar
350g/12oz sugar
3 level tablespoons pickling spice

Prepare the samphire by removing the tender shoots from any of the more woody stems. Soak the tender shoots in cold water for an hour and finally rinse off by placing them in a colander and flushing them under cold running water. Chop into 5cm/2in lengths.

Into four sterlized storage jars place four of the garlic cloves and a tablespoon of pickling spice. Add the lengths of samphire until each jar is full.

Put the remainder of the ingredients into a pan and bring the mixture to the boil before allowing it to simmer for approximately quarter of an hour.

Then (making sure to leave a little air space at the top of each jar), pour the liquid over the samphire, spices and garlic cloves. Seal whilst still hot. The pickled samphire can be eaten after about a week; however, the longer it is stored, the more flavoursome it will become.

Pickled Magnolia Flowers

Yes, really! We discovered this quite fascinating recipe on an equally fascinating website, which can be accessed at www.EatWeeds.co.uk. It is the brainchild of Robin Harford, who is based in Devon and is passionate about extolling the virtues of utilizing the best of what nature has to offer. Robin runs regular foraging courses, in which he teaches those who would like to know more exactly how to go about getting the most from the countryside's seasonal harvests. This is his own recipe and we are very grateful to Robin for giving us permission to include it here.

Robin says that the flowers of the *Magnolia denudata* are exquisite to taste. 'The texture and taste is nothing less than Love Food. Every person that has tasted this recipe remarks on how amazing the magnolia flowers are. Although the end result looks like pickled oysters in malt vinegar, the flavour will convert you as soon as it hits your taste buds.' The quantities given should, according to Robin, make about one cup (assuming the American usage of 'cup' as a cooking measurement, this should equate to roughly 225g/8oz).

450g/1lb fresh young magnolia flowers that
    have been separated
1 teaspoon salt

1½ cups (approx 375ml/12fl oz) rice vinegar*
1 cup (approx 225g/8oz) sugar

Wash and dry the magnolia flowers with paper towels and put them in a sterilized jar along with the salt.

Mix the rice vinegar and sugar in a pan and bring to a boil. Pour the hot mixture of vinegar and sugar over the magnolia flowers.

Allow to cool, then screw a cap on the jar. Eat the Pickled Magnolia Flowers either when cold, or as an accompaniment to salads.

* Author's Note: rice vinegar is higher in vinegar content than the norm, but has the great advantage of being less acidic, therefore, milder and sweeter. It is available in most supermarkets.

Pickled Spice Pears

Suitable as an accompaniment to Sunday's leftover cold roast, pickled pears also work well with a summer salad. As should always be the aim, this is a good way of preserving and subsequently using up a glut of early autumn fruit from the orchard, whilst ensuring that nothing goes to waste. This, and the recipe for Damson Sauce, are courtesy of Michael Stamford, who runs a small organic fruit orchard near Stow-on-the-Wold, Gloucestershire.

2kg/4lb 6oz pears, peeled, cored and halved	2 teaspoons cardamom pods, split
30ml/1fl oz lemon juice	2 teaspoons black peppercorns, coarsely
water, for poaching the pears	crushed in a pestle and mortar
1kg/2lb 3oz sugar	3 bay leaves
700ml/1¼fl oz red wine vinegar	rind of one orange

Place the pear halves into a preserving pan, add the lemon juice and top up with water until the pan is half filled. Bring the water to the boil before turning the heat down to simmer. Cook the pears for about a quarter of an hour, or until soft without becoming mushy. Drain the pears and put to one side.

In the same pan, pour in the vinegar and add the sugar and the spices. Add the bay leaves and three broad strips of orange peel cut from the rind. Boil all the ingredients until the sugar has completely dissolved. Bring the pears back to the pan and simmer in the liquid for a further ten minutes (periodically, gently turn the pears to ensure that all sides are cooked and thoroughly infused with the vinegar/sugar/spice mix).

Using a slotted spoon, place the pear halves into three warmed and sterilized medium-sized preserving jars, making sure to include a piece of orange rind and a bay leaf in each. Pour the liquid from the pan into the jars, making sure that all the fruit is properly covered. Seal whilst warm but leave to cool before storing. Pickled properly, Michael says that the fruit will keep for up to three months.

Making Pickled Spice Pears is just one way of preserving and subsequently using up a glut of early autumn fruit from the orchard.

PICKLED SHALLOTS

If you can find small 'button' onions, they work equally as well, but, from personal experience, we much prefer the extra crispness of a pickled shallot – can there be many things better than the crunch and spiced vinegar sensation after biting into a pickled shallot that has been maturing for several months? Weights and quantities are difficult for this traditional country recipe, as much depends on how many shallots you have and how fond you are of pickled onions!

Before peeling the shallots, soak them overnight in a brine (see Chapter 3) made up of 115g/4oz salt to every 1.2ltr/2pt of water. Peel and soak them in a fresh brine for a couple of days before draining and packing in jars, which are then filled with spiced vinegar (see Chapter 3 or Index), to which a small amount of sugar has been added. Seal tightly with non-metallic lids (the vinegar will corrode them) and leave for several months.

NB: There are probably as many different recipes for pickling shallots and onions as there are people who make them. Some of them will tell you to forgo the overnight soaking in brine, for example, or to add dried chillies, cloves and other various possibilities to the shallots whilst bottling. Rather than just listen to one, prepare all your shallots by peeling and soaking in brine as described above and then, into each jar or bottle, experiment by adding some of their suggestions – it would be a shame to prepare the whole of one season's batch in a uniform way only to discover that your personal tastes are not the same as those who recommended the recipe. Remember to label each jar carefully and include what has been added to each, so that, in the future, you can replicate the one most favoured by you and your friends and family.

Shallots in Balsamic Vinegar

A very simple recipe, this is actually nothing more than glorified pickled onions – but what a difference the inclusion of balsamic, rather than 'normal' pickling, vinegar makes! Balsamic vinegar is Italian in origin (the very best coming from Modena in the north of the country) and is made by boiling down grape pressings until they turns into a rich, dark syrup. This syrup is then placed into oak barrels and a vinegar 'mother' is added in order to help start the necessary aging process. As it matures, the balsamic vinegar is moved into ever smaller barrels variously made from the wood of chestnut, cherry, ash, mulberry and juniper. All of these woods add taste and, as the liquid ages, more and more moisture is lost – further thickening the vinegar and concentrating the intensity of flavour.

500g/1lb 2oz shallots, peeled but whole
2 tablespoons muscovado sugar

a few sprigs of either fresh thyme or rosemary
300ml/10fl oz balsamic vinegar

Pickled Shallots.

Place the sugar, herbs and vinegar into a heavy-bottomed pan and bring the mixture to the boil. Add the shallots, cover the pan and simmer gently for thirty to forty-five minutes, or until the shallots feel tender when tested with the point of a sharp knife.

Spoon and pour all the pan ingredients into a warm, clean jar before sealing tightly. Allow to cool and then store for at least four weeks before eating.

NB: One way of peeling shallots without losing several layers of 'flesh' is to place them in a bowl, cover them with boiling water and then allow them to steep for two or three minutes. This has the effect of loosening the skin.

Pickled Cucumbers

Traditionally, outdoor, or 'ridge', cucumbers are short and dumpy and covered with nodules and bumps. Some of the older varieties might still be like this, but it is nowadays possible to grow perfect outdoor cucumbers that look every bit as appetizing as their greenhouse-grown cousins. Short or long, lumpy or smooth, outdoor cucumbers are perfect for pick-

Pickled Cucumbers.

ling. Use the youngest available and do nothing more in their preparation than wipe them clean, cut them in half and then into quarters. There's no need to peel them.

1kg/2lb 3oz outdoor cucumbers	55g/2oz white sugar
1ltr/1¾pt water	1ltr/1¾pt pickling vinegar
175g/6oz salt	bay leaves – one for each jar of pickled cucumber

Boil the water and salt, then put aside until the liquid is cooled, before pouring over the cucumber quarters. Leave for a day.

In a saucepan, gently heat the sugar and pickling vinegar until the sugar has completely dissolved. Drain and rinse the cucumbers under running cold water and leave to dry off for a couple of hours.

Place into clean, sterile jars and cover with the vinegar/sugar mix before adding a bay leaf and sealing securely.

PICKLED GHERKINS

Love them or hate them, it would be remiss of us not to include gherkins, a member of the cucumber family. Wash the fruits and rub with a cloth to dry and remove any 'prickles'. Place them in a bowl and cover with salt for twenty-four hours.

Rinse thoroughly and drain before packing them into sterile jars. Cover the gherkins with warm malt pickling vinegar and add half a teaspoon of dill seed to each jar before sealing with an air-tight lid.

To achieve a bright green colour to your gherkins, some recipes suggest that you should cover them with plain boiling vinegar and leave for a day before draining off the vinegar, reboiling it and doing the same thing again several times until the gherkins are bright green.

Drain off the boiled vinegar, pack the gherkins into jars in the normal way and cover with cold spiced vinegar before sealing the lids tightly.

PICKLED PEPPERS

Quite why Peter Piper ever decided to 'pick a peck of pickled peppers', we've no idea. The method of pickling peppers was, however, described as far back as 1824 by Mary Randolph in her book *The Virginia Housewife*:

Gather the large bell pepper when quite young, leave the seeds in and the stem on, cut a slit in one side, between the large veins, to let the water in; pour boiling salt and water on, changing it every day for three weeks – you must keep them closely stopped; if, at the end of this time, they be a good green, put them in pots and cover them with cold vinegar and a little turmeric; those that are not sufficiently green, must be continued under the same process till they are so. Be careful not to cut through the large veins, as the heat will instantly diffuse itself through the pod.

Pickled Eggs

Pickled eggs are excellent served as an hors d'oeuvre and, for something a little different, quails' eggs can be substituted for ordinary chicken's eggs (increase the egg quantity to twenty-four).

14 hard-boiled eggs	1 tablespoon white pepper
1.2ltr/2pt white malt vinegar	1 dessertspoon whole allspice
1 root ginger	3 red or green chillies

For the spiced vinegar, tie the spices in a piece of muslin and boil gently in the white malt vinegar for five minutes. Pour into a bowl and leave to cool.

Peel the eggs and pack into wide-necked jars with a piece or two of chilli in each jar. Fill with the cold vinegar to cover the eggs completely. Seal and leave for one month before eating.

Pickle and preserve any surfeit of free-range eggs laid by your chickens. (Photo courtesy of Rupert Stephenson)

PICKLE-RELATED FACTS AND TRIVIA FROM AROUND THE WORLD

- More than half the cucumbers grown in the United States are made into pickles and it is estimated that the average American eats 8½lb of pickles a year.
- 40 per cent of all pickles produced in North America during World War II were kept aside for use by its Armed Forces.
- According to Pickle Packers International Inc., the perfect pickle should show seven warts per square inch for North American tastes – Europeans prefer wartless pickles. The company also claims that you should be able to hear the crunch of a good pickled onion from ten paces away when it is being bitten into!
- The number '57' on the Heinz ketchup bottle is thought to represent the number of varieties of pickles and produce the company once manufactured.
- In years gone by, because fresh fruits and vegetables were hard to come by, sailors, armies and travellers took pickles with them; not only were they an excellent source of vitamin C, they also helped to prevent scurvy.
- Pickling has been used to preserve food for almost 5,000 years.
- In 2,030BC, cucumbers native to India were brought to the Tigris Valley where they were first preserved and eaten as pickles.
- Various Roman emperors, including Julius Caesar and Tiberius, ate pickles on a daily or regular basis, believing that they had health-giving properties.
- Cleopatra was apparently a fan of pickles, believing that they enhanced her beauty – she would, we think, have found it more pleasant to have stuck with her baths of asses' milk!
- Queen Elizabeth I was another famous lady pickle eater.
- Samuel Pepys' diary mentions a glass of pickled gherkins as being something to be highly prized.
- The expression 'to be in a pickle' is thought to have been first used by William Shakespeare in his play *The Tempest* where he wrote 'How camest thou in this pickle?'
- In Germany, there is a tradition whereby a glass pickle is hidden in the tree on Christmas Eve and whoever finds it receives a special present.
- Frenchman Nicholas Appert is thought to have been the first person to begin packing pickles in jars for commercial sale. His 'factory' began in 1820.
- Traditionally, homemade pickles were packed in earthenware crocks, whilst chutneys and relishes were kept in glass jars.
- Kosher pickles can only be truly 'kosher' if prepared in the presence of a Rabbi.
- And finally, scraping the bottom of the barrel (whether a pickle one or not) in connection with related trivia, John Lennon's first girlfriend was named Thelma Pickles!

Recipes for Relishes, Ketchups, Marinades and Dips

Relishes are made in different ways throughout the world: some are a sort of hybrid between chutneys and pickles, cooked, puréed and thickened, whilst others are nothing more than extremely finely chopped raw vegetables and herbs. They might be creamy, as when mixed with yoghurt, or they might be spicy and sharp as a result of having had vinegar added. Generally, however, relishes are vegetables or fruit preserved in vinegar, salt and spice. For one reason or another – sometimes as a result of 'thinning' – some chutneys and pickles become technically a relish or sauce. Or even a 'salsa' – which is simply a Spanish word for 'sauce'. Conversely, a relish that combines hot, sour, sweet and spice flavours is often called a chutney – no wonder we suggested at the outset that true definitions for each are so interchangeable! Most of the relishes in this chapter are ready to serve straight away.

Chilli Jam Relish

Time-consuming to make perhaps, but definitely well worth all the effort in the end!

1kg/2lb 3oz ripe tomatoes, roughly chopped
4 red bird's eye chillies, deseeded
4 green finger chillies, deseeded
1 Scotch bonnet chilli (very hot!), deseeded
4 garlic cloves, peeled
5cm/2in piece fresh root ginger

2 tablespoons Thai fish sauce
2 red bell peppers, deseeded and chopped
450g/1lb soft brown sugar
6 tablespoons red wine vinegar
1 teaspoon tamarind paste

Place half the quantity of tomatoes into a blender, together with the chillies, garlic cloves, ginger, fish sauce, tamarind paste and red peppers. Blend until a thick paste is achieved and pour into a pan with the sugar and vinegar. Slowly bring to the boil, stirring all the time, removing any 'scum' that may appear.

Chilli Jam Relish.

Pulse the remaining tomatoes into a chunky pulp; add to the pan, return to the boil and then simmer for about two hours, or until thick. It is important to stir frequently throughout the entire process.

Pot into warm sterile jars; cover tightly and label.

Beetroot Relish

This recipe first appeared in print in 1978 as a contribution made by Doreen Allars of Welbourne, Lincolnshire to *Farmhouse Kitchen II*. According to Doreen Allars the relish 'keeps for about a month, preferably in the fridge' and is 'easier to make in small quantities'.

450g/1lb beetroot
225g/8oz horseradish
115g/4oz demerara sugar

300ml/10fl oz wine, or cider vinegar
pinch of salt

Wash the beetroot without damaging the skin and either boil in water, or cook in a pressure cooker. Meanwhile, wash the horseradish and grate it across the sticks ('It is a good idea to do this out of doors or near an open window, as it will make you "cry" ').

Peel and shred the cooked beetroot on the coarse side of a grater.
Mix all the ingredients together and pack into jars with vinegar-proof lids.

NB: This relish is ready to eat immediately.

Beetroot and Cabbage Relish

Beetroot and Cabbage Relish marries well with terrines, as well as pâtés and cold meats.

1kg/2lb 3oz beetroot, raw, peeled and coarsely grated
55g/2oz horseradish root, grated
1.5kg/3lb 5oz cabbage, coarsely chopped
450g/1lb onions, peeled and coarsely chopped

450g/1lb white sugar
500ml/16fl oz red wine vinegar
14g/½oz salt

Cook all the ingredients together in a large, heavy-bottomed pan for about twenty minutes or until the mixture has thickened.

Carrot and Almond Relish

Based on an old Middle Eastern recipe for carrot jam called 'angel's hair' (often used to complement curries), this recipe appears to have been adapted and developed by professional chefs and amateur cooks alike. It goes well with cheese and both hot and cold meats.

500g/1lb 2oz carrots, coarsely grated
15g/½oz coriander seeds, crushed in a pestle and mortar
55g/2oz fresh ginger, finely grated
200g/7oz caster sugar
125ml/4fl oz white wine vinegar

30ml/1fl oz clear honey
1½ teaspoons salt
rind of a lemon, finely grated
55g/2oz flaked almonds

Put the grated carrot, crushed coriander seeds, finely grated ginger and sugar into a heavy-bottomed preserving pan and fold all the ingredients together with a spoon.

In a measuring jug, place the vinegar, honey and salt and stir until the salt has dissolved. Pour the liquid over the contents of the pan and allow to marinade for about an hour.

Afterwards, bring to the boil, then simmer gently until the carrots and ginger are almost soft. Stir in the lemon rind and continue simmering until the mixture has thickened. Using a wooden spoon, stir the relish towards the end of cooking in order to prevent it catching and burning on the bottom of the pan (remember that you are cooking with comparatively small amounts of liquid in this recipe).

In a frying pan, dry-roast the almonds until they begin to colour, then carefully fold them into the pan mixture.

Spoon into warm sterilized jars; cover and seal. Store for at least a week and up to a year.

A wooden spoon is essential when making all manner of relishes and ketchups.

Gooseberry, Orange and Pistachio Relish

A gooseberry-based sauce or relish of any kind has, certainly since the 1500s and prob-ably long before that, been used as an accompaniment to oily fish such as mackerel, or spooned next to rich and often greasy meat such as goose. Perhaps now is the time to revive the custom?

1.5kg/3lb 5oz gooseberries, washed, topped and tailed
grated peel and juice of 4 large oranges
300ml/10fl oz water

1.5kg/3lb 5oz sugar
175g/6oz fresh pistachio nuts (unsalted), roughly chopped

Into a preserving pan place the gooseberries and grated orange rind, together with the water. Simmer slowly for ten minutes, then add both the sugar and orange juice. Bring to the boil and cook until the mixture begins to thicken and set (it should have the appear-ance of a jam or marmalade rather than a chutney or pickle).

Once the mixture has set, remove the pan from the heat and stir in the pistachio nuts. Spoon into sterilized jars and seal tightly whilst the relish is still hot.

Onion Relish

Beryl Woodhouse, of Staffordshire – one of our kindly hosts as we travelled around Britain in connection with our book, *The New Country Cook* (Crowood, 2009) – gave us this recipe for an onion-lover's relish, saying that 'it should be stored in the fridge and will keep for about a month'.

700g/1½lb onions, peeled and sliced thinly
125g/4½oz butter
salt and pepper

175g/6oz sugar
100ml/3½fl oz red wine vinegar
225ml/8fl oz red wine

Heat the butter in a pan and, once it has melted, cook it for a minute or two without letting it brown and burn. Add the onions and a little seasoning.

Stir in the sugar and mix well before simmering for thirty to thirty-five minutes with the pan lid covering.

Stir in the vinegar and red wine and cook for another half an hour, this time with the lid off.

Stir frequently at this stage and when thickened, ladle into warmed, sterilized jars and cover immediately.

Sweet Pepper Relish

Eat this straight away or store it in a sealed container in the fridge for a few days – you could try bottling it as for chutney, but it will not keep for any length of time.

Sweet Red Pepper relish in the making!

6 large green peppers
6 large red peppers
6 medium-sized onions, peeled
boiling water (for blanching)

700ml/1¼pt white malt, or white wine, vinegar
1 rounded tablespoon salt
275g/10½oz granulated sugar
1 rounded teaspoon mustard seed

Split the peppers and remove the seeds. Finely chop the pepper flesh and the onions.

Put these into a bowl for blanching; pour on enough boiling water to cover and drain immediately. Place the vegetables into a pan and cover with cold water, bring to the boil and drain again, leaving them for the time being in a colander.

Put the vinegar, salt, sugar and mustard seed into the pan and bring to the boil. Once the pepper/onion mixture has thoroughly drained, stir it into the hot vinegar and simmer for twenty to twenty-five minutes, or until it is fairly thick.

Easy Balsamic and Tomato Relish

If you're ever in a hurry and need a relish to accompany a beefburger, this takes but seconds to do.

4 tinned plum tomatoes
6 tablespoons balsamic vinegar

4 tablespoons dark brown sugar

In a bowl, bind together the tomatoes, vinegar and sugar – there, told you it was easy!

Easy Balsamic and Tomato Relish – in this case, set alongside an ostrich steak bun!

Cranberry, Orange and Vodka Relish

Here is yet another quick and easy 'cheat' – it takes no time at all to prepare and goes extremely well with the Christmas turkey.

285g/10oz tub fresh cranberry sauce   small piece of fresh ginger
1 orange (keep the zest), segmented   1 'shot' of vodka

In a saucepan, heat the cranberry sauce, orange zest, ginger and vodka. Simmer for five minutes before removing the pan from the heat, removing the ginger and adding the orange segments. Allow to cool, but not go cold (room temperature, is ideal).

Chris and Felicity's Celery and Fennel Relish

Devised to be eaten either hot or cold, this recipe was supplied by Chris and Felicity Stockwell who tell us that, if you choose to use it cold, store it in the fridge and don't keep it any longer than three days.

4 good-sized celery sticks, finely chopped   4 tablespoons olive oil
1 small bulb of fennel, finely chopped   juice of a half orange
1 small onion, peeled and finely chopped   2 tablespoons white wine vinegar
1 clove garlic, peeled and crushed   2 teaspoons Dijon mustard

In a frying pan heat the oil and sweat down the celery, fennel, onion and garlic until soft and slightly translucent.

Pour in the orange, vinegar and mustard, stir and bring up the heat until the liquid is boiling.

Finally, spoon the relish from the pan and into a small serving dish.

Quick Cranberry Relish

Perhaps best known in America for its use when accompanying thick slices of leftover cold turkey, cranberry relish can, nevertheless, also be utilized along with cold game.

500ml/18fl oz homemade cranberry sauce (made in advance)	¼ teaspoon cinnamon
225g/8oz tin pineapple chunks, drained and roughly mashed	pinch of ground cloves
55g/2oz pecan nuts, chopped	

Combine all the ingredients together in a bowl and serve immediately.

To make the Cranberry Sauce:

350g/12oz frozen cranberries	250ml/8fl oz water
225g/8oz granulated sugar	

Put the sugar and water into a pan and bring to the boil, taking care that the sugar does not stick before dissolving.

Add the cranberries and bring back to the boil. Reduce the heat and cook gently for ten minutes, stirring from time to time.

Cover, cool and then place in the fridge until such time as it is needed.

NB: Any leftover sauce could be used as a topping for a bowl of vanilla ice cream or Greek yoghurt. If it is intended only as an ingredient to the relish, then, as an experiment (depending on personal taste), try including a tablespoon of horseradish sauce to your mix.

Rhubarb Relish

Although its most common use is in crumbles and puddings, rhubarb is actually a vegetable. Like cranberries, it is almost too 'tart' to eat without the addition of a sweetener such as fruit juice, honey or sugar. Choose stalks that are firm and avoid including any part of the leaves, as they are toxic – although you'd have to eat quite a bit before feeling ill. Rhubarb relish goes well with cold roast beef and pork.

450g/1lb rhubarb stems, cut into 2.5cm/1in pieces	1 tablespoon salt
2 large onions, peeled and thinly sliced	¼ teaspoon (or a little more) cayenne
2 teaspoons curry powder	125ml/4fl oz vinegar
4 tablespoons sugar	

Include only perfect, unblemished sticks of rhubarb when making Rhubarb Relish.

Place all the ingredients together in a heavy-bottomed pan and, over a low heat, cook the mixture until the rhubarb begins to soften and release its natural juices, then boil it rapidly until the onions are soft.

Bottle, seal and store for up to a month.

NB: For a hotter relish, add mustard to taste. For a sweeter one, double the amount of sugar and add 450g/1lb of chopped seedless raisins.

Walnut and Coriander Relish

Very definitely Indian in origin, this is an excellent accompaniment to curry. It is best eaten as soon as possible after making, but, as it only takes a few minutes from start to finish, can be easily fabricated whilst the main dishes are cooking.

115g/4oz walnuts, shelled and finely chopped in a food processor
6 tablespoons fresh coriander, chopped

juice of half a lemon
¼ teaspoon cayenne pepper
4 tablespoons natural yoghurt

Add together all the ingredients and work into a paste (quantities given should be sufficient to make approximately 225g/8oz of relish).

Greek Relish

Given to us by restaurateur Alexios Theophilus, this relish is best described as being a type of mayonnaise made without eggs and, according to Alexios, goes well with fish dishes, or as an accompaniment to salads.

single thick slice of stale white bread
(approximately 5cm/2in in thickness)
4 garlic cloves, peeled then pulped with a
large pestle and mortar

115g/4oz almonds, blanched and grated
125g/4fl oz olive oil (Greek, of course!)
white wine vinegar, to taste
salt, to season

Remove the crust from the bread and soak it in water before squeezing out the surplus.

Add the soaked bread to the pulped garlic, then (in small, gradual amounts) the grated almonds, slowly working them together with the pestle and mortar until a paste is achieved.

Begin adding the olive oil, drop by drop, until the paste is such that you can add the remainder at a 'normal' speed (in much the same way as one would if adding oil to eggs to make a conventional mayonnaise). Season to taste with the salt and white wine vinegar.

Field Mushroom Relish

Bottled and stored, this relish will keep for a month. Alternatively, keep it in a container in the fridge for two weeks or, better still, eat it straight away!

225g/8oz large field mushrooms, wiped clean and finely chopped
1 onion, peeled and finely chopped
1 garlic clove, peeled and finely chopped
3 tablespoons olive oil

6 tablespoons red wine vinegar
4 tablespoons fresh parsley, finely chopped
½ teaspoon black peppercorns, crushed in a pestle and mortar

Heat the oil in a pan over a low ring and soften the onions and garlic without burning.

Increase the heat to a medium setting; pour in the vinegar and let it come up to boil before adding the mushrooms, parsley and crushed peppercorns. Immediately after the mixture has boiled again, lower the heat and simmer (without the pan lid) for about ten minutes.

If intending to use the relish straight away, allow it to cool before serving. If it is to be stored, place it into a warmed (warming the jar will prevent the glass from cracking) sterilized jar immediately after cooking and seal the top straight away.

Cabbage Coleslaw

Nowadays a part of everyday living, coleslaw can be made in many ways. It can quite reasonably be construed as a type of relish, so we've decided to include three variations in this section.

1 large carrot, peeled and grated
150g/5½oz white cabbage, finely shredded
1 tablespoon extra virgin olive oil
4 tablespoons low-fat yogurt

pinch white pepper
1 apple, cored and diced
1 tablespoon cider vinegar
1 tablespoon walnut pieces

Mix together the carrot, cabbage, olive oil, yogurt and pepper. Mix the diced apple with the cider vinegar and leave for a minute or two in order to prevent the apple from turning brown.

Finally, excepting the walnuts, bring all the ingredients together and leave to 'mature' for about a quarter of an hour. Add the walnuts just before serving.

NB: If you are making this in the autumn or winter and have fresh leeks around, try adding half a shredded leek to the initial mix.

Broccolislaw

As an alternative to the type of coleslaw that has cabbage as its main ingredient, try this made with the head of fresh broccoli.

4 slices of back bacon, coarsely chopped and fried until crispy
1 broccoli head, stems trimmed and the florets cut into small pieces
½ medium-sized red onion, peeled and finely diced
425g/15oz tin sliced water chestnuts, rinsed and coarsely chopped

60ml/2fl oz plain yoghurt
60ml/2fl oz mayonnaise
45ml/1½fl oz cider vinegar
2 teaspoons sugar
½ teaspoon salt
ground pepper, to taste

Place the yoghurt, mayonnaise, cider vinegar, sugar and salt and pepper into a mixing bowl and beat together until creamy.

Add the broccoli pieces, bacon, chopped onion and chestnuts, mixing them well in so that each piece is thoroughly coated with the mixture.

Cover with cling-film, chill and keep in the fridge until needed (it can be kept safely for up to forty-eight hours).

Caulislaw with Dreamy, Creamy Dressing

Another alternative to using cabbage in coleslaw: you could, in fact, try experimenting and combining broccoli florets with the cauliflower heads. Cooking in all its guises is, to a large extent, all about using your imagination.

1 cauliflower head, with the florets cut or broken into small pieces
1 large red pepper, roasted, peeled, deseeded and finely chopped
½ medium-sized red onion, peeled and finely chopped

for the Dreamy, Creamy Dressing
125ml/4fl oz mayonnaise
60ml/2fl oz sour cream
30ml/1fl oz lemon juice

½ teaspoon salt
¼ teaspoon dried dill weed (the leaf and stem; sometimes referred to as leaf dill)

Steam the cauliflower florets until *al dente* before placing them under a running cold water tap in a colander. Leave to drain before then placing them and the pepper and onion into a mixing bowl.

Make the dressing by mixing together all the ingredients and then pour over the cauliflower mixture, folding in well to ensure that the florets, onion and red pepper pieces are all well coated.

Cover with cling-film, chill and keep in the fridge until needed – do not keep for more than forty-eight hours.

Pistachio and Sesame Seed Cream

Not quite a relish and not quite ketchup, Pistachio and Sesame Seed Cream is perhaps more of a sauce. It is, however, far too good not to be included here! The thickness of the 'cream' is dictated by personal preference and the length of time you choose to cook it. Use it spooned over green vegetables such as runner beans, or very lightly steamed cabbage.

115g/4oz blanched, toasted and ground raw pistachios
½ tablespoon sesame seeds
80ml/2½fl oz melted, unsalted butter
1 teaspoon black mustard seeds
1 teaspoon green chillies, deseeded and minced

500ml/18fl oz double cream
¼ teaspoon turmeric
1 teaspoon ground coriander
½ teaspoon salt
¼ teaspoon ground white pepper
2 tablespoons fresh coriander, very finely chopped or minced

Having melted the butter in a heavy-bottomed pan over a low heat, drop in the mustard seeds and gently fry until you can hear them popping.

Add the sesame seeds and green chillies, stirring continuously until the sesame seeds have darkened in colour.

Add the pistachio nuts, cream, turmeric and ground coriander. Increase the heat and, still stirring, bring the mixture to the boil before then simmering until the cream mixture is thick enough to coat the back of your wooden spoon (this might take about quarter of an hour).

Finally, add the salt, pepper and fresh coriander before serving immediately over your green vegetable dish.

A preserving pan and set of non-metallic spoons are gifts that will be much appreciated by would-be chutney, relish and ketchup makers!

KETCHUPS

No need at all to settle for supermarket-bought ketchups, although it must be admitted that there are some very interesting and tasty varieties on offer. But how much better to make one's own using surplus stock from the garden, purchased locally from the nearest farmers' market, or even gathered as a result of a weekend trip into the countryside! Fortunately, we are sailing in safer waters when it comes to describing the exact definition of ketchup – whereas some chutneys, pickles and relishes become a 'crossover' of meanings, ketchup is, according to the *Oxford English Dictionary*, 'a spicy sauce made from tomatoes, mushrooms, vinegar, etc., used as a condiment'.

Mushroom Ketchup

The gastronomic possibilities of mushrooms are enormous for chefs with imagination and good culinary taste. Whatever you do with them, it is always recommended that you clean them either with a fine-edged knife or a slightly damp cloth, rather than immersing or washing them under a direct flow of water.

900g/2lb mushrooms, peeled and sliced
250ml/8fl oz water
1 bay leaf
250ml/8fl oz vinegar

3 teaspoons salt
1½ teaspoons powdered cinnamon
¼ teaspoon each of cayenne, ground cloves
    and mace

Together with the water and bay leaf, place the mushrooms in a pan and cook for half an hour, or until they are quite soft.

Rub the resultant purée through a sieve and add to them the remainder of the ingredients. Cook for a further thirty minutes over a moderate heat.

Allow to cool before bottling.

Apple Ketchup

Take careful note of the method for this one, as actual quantities of all the remaining ingredients vary depending on how much pulp is recovered from the apples.

12 cooking apples, peeled, cored and quartered
medium-sized onions, peeled and grated
sugar
salt

powdered cinnamon
mustard powder
ground cloves

Place the apples in a pan with enough water to cover them and simmer until soft and almost all the water has evaporated.

Rub the mixture through a sieve and measure the pulp. To each 1.2ltr/2pt of pulp add 500ml/16fl oz of vinegar, two grated onions, 115g/4oz sugar, three teaspoons of salt, two of powdered cinnamon and one teaspoon each of mustard powder and cloves.

Bring the ketchup to the boil and simmer for an hour.

Pour into bottles or jars.

WALNUT KETCHUP

In France, walnut trees are quite common. This ketchup is traditional, time-consuming and rather tasty!

Select 100 young green walnuts, gathered before the enclosing nutshells harden, using all the fruit.

Bruise them slightly and place in an earthenware crock with six tablespoons of salt and 2.5ltr/4pt of vinegar before leaving them for eight days (not a week; not ten days, nor a fortnight, but for exactly eight!), stirring and crushing daily with a wooden spoon.

Drain the liquid into a pan and add to it 115g/4oz anchovies, 12 finely chopped shallots, one tablespoon of grated horseradish and half a teaspoon each of ground mace, ground ginger, ground cloves, pepper, and 250ml/8fl oz of port wine. Simmer gently for three-quarters of an hour and allow to cool.

Strain and pour into bottles. Store for several weeks before using.

Elderberry Ketchup

In nineteenth-century cookbooks this was quite often referred to either as 'pontac', or 'pontack' ketchup.

1ltr/1¾pt ripe elderberries, stripped from their
    stalks and thoroughly washed
700ml/1¼pt vinegar
125ml/4fl oz anchovy sauce
8 shallots, peeled and chopped
5 cloves

1 teaspoon black peppercorns
2 blades mace
2.5cm/1in piece ginger, gently bruised with the
    aid of a rolling pin or meat mallet
salt to taste

Carefully boil the vinegar. Place the elderberries into an ovenproof dish; pour over the boiling vinegar and place the dish into the oven (set at low to medium) for about two and a half hours (or until all the elderberry juice has been released).

Strain off the liquid (but do not press the berries, otherwise you will end up with the skin and 'pips' in the finished ketchup) and place into a heavy-bottomed saucepan along with the remainder of the ingredients. Boil for several minutes, taste (add more anchovy sauce, or salt if required), strain and bottle.

NB: In the original cookbooks, boned anchovy fillets were used, but anchovy sauce is an acceptable and far easier alternative. Exact quantities should be experimented with and will obviously depend on how keen you are on the 'saltiness' of anchovies!

Homemade tomato ketchup, as shown here, has a totally different taste, texture and colour to those that are commercially produced.

Blackfriars Tomato Ketchup

Andy Hook is the owner of *Blackfriars Restaurant*, which is, appropriately enough, situated on Friars Street in Newcastle. Andy and his team specialize in what he describes as 'classic but gutsy British food using fresh, local and seasonal produce'. Andy is a member of the Slow Food organization, which celebrates the pleasures of the table and appreciates a slow approach towards cooking and eating as opposed to the 'fast food' culture of the last twenty years or so. He was kind enough to assist us in producing *The New Country Cook* (Crowood, 2009) and has helped us again by submitting this particular recipe.

5kg/11lb mixed ripe English tomatoes
2 teaspoons salt, to taste
pepper, to taste
60ml/2fl oz rapeseed oil for frying
5 large onions, peeled and finely diced
5 garlic cloves, peeled and finely diced
150g/6oz brown sugar

300ml/10fl oz cider vinegar
3–4 teaspoons pickling spice (or a half
   teaspoon each of coriander seed,
   cinnamon, cloves, mace, black
   peppercorns, dried chilli flakes and mustard
   seeds, tied up in muslin)
2 bay leaves

Halve the tomatoes, season with salt and pepper; lay them out in a warm oven with the door ajar for twelve to twenty-four hours until dry and sticky.

Using a heavy-bottomed pan, softly fry the onions for a few minutes before adding the garlic. Add the tomatoes and gently cook until soft (about half an hour).

Push through a sieve into a pan; add the sugar, vinegar and spices. Cook very gently for another hour (adding water if the mixture becomes too dry and starts to catch).

Remove the muslin spice bag and bay leaves before storing.

Damson Sauce

This recipe suggests the use of damsons, but red plums would do equally as well. It is another recipe from Michael Stamford (*see also* Pickled Spice Pears), who says that 'the whole point of making pickles and chutneys is to use up whatever is readily and locally available – so don't get hung up about using exactly what any recipe states and use your imagination to find suitable workable alternatives'.

450g/1lb damsons, destoned and roughly
   chopped
125ml/4fl oz dry sherry (plus a further 'glug'
   for finishing off before sealing)
30ml/1fl oz sherry vinegar
175g/6oz brown sugar

1 garlic clove, peeled and crushed
2.5cm/1in piece fresh root ginger, finely
   chopped
pinch of salt
3–4 drops Tabasco sauce

Place the damsons into a heavy-bottomed saucepan and add both the sherry and sherry vinegar. Very gently, bring the damson mixture to the boil and then just as soon as it has, reduce the heat and cover the pan before allowing the contents to simmer for ten minutes (or until the damsons are soft).

Damsons and plums are useful ingredients when making a sweet-tasting sauce.

Next, push the mixture through a sieve in order to hold back the stones and skin.

Place the resultant purée back into the pan and add the sugar, garlic, finely chopped ginger and salt. Increase the heat until all the sugar has dissolved and the purée just comes to the boil. Simmer (uncovered) for a further fifteen minutes or so, or until the sauce begins to thicken.

Finally, remove the pan from the heat and stir in the Tabasco sauce.

Spoon into warmed, sterilized jars and add a little 'glug' of sherry before sealing.

NB: Once cooled, store in the fridge (rather than the pantry), where it will keep for at least a month if left unopened.

MARINADES

As the origins of some relishes undoubtedly lay in the fact that they were used as a rubbed or brushed-on addition to meats due to be cooked over an open flame, it is but a short step to marinades, which also help to break down meat fibres, as well as imbibing them with subtle tastes. They also counteract the possibility of dryness as the meat cooks. In other cases, a marinade might be used to coagulate the protein in fish that is to be eaten raw – a system, according to Tom Stobart in *The Cook's Encyclopaedia*, somewhat akin to 'chemical cooking'.

Meat joints should be left in a marinade for at least twelve hours in order to bring out the best flavours. Remember to turn the meat occasionally during that time. It may be that some joints and whole game birds are too big to be totally immersed in a marinade – unless you were to mix up such a quantity that it would become very expensive and wasteful. In such cases, the easiest way of ensuring that the meat has received its full share of marinade is to place it and the mixture into a strong plastic bag and securely tie the neck. Then, it is a simple matter to turn the bag over periodically.

MARINADES

There is no exact science to preparing a marinade and a typical one that will work well with 'heavier' meats such as game or beef is likely to combine some, or all of the following ingredients:

- a bottle of red wine (full-bodied rather than the lighter Gamay grape type)
- two tablespoons of red wine vinegar (or rather less of balsamic)
- chopped onion and garlic
- herbs
- a pinch of mixed dried spices
- a pinch of grated nutmeg
- a bay leaf or two
- a couple of 'glugs' of olive oil
- and, if you can get them, half a dozen juniper berries.

NB: There is a school of thought amongst some professional chefs that the wine only serves to pickle the meat and, in doing so, actually draws out some of the moisture. You may prefer to follow their advice and omit all but the slightest amount of wine, replacing it with rather more olive oil.

Ginger and Garlic Marinade

For lighter meats such as partridge and rabbit, a ginger and garlic marinade gives an almost oriental combination, especially if a small amount of soy sauce is added.

1 onion, peeled and finely chopped	125ml/4fl oz lemon juice
2 garlic cloves, peeled and crushed	125ml/4fl oz sesame oil
1 tablespoon ginger, freshly grated	2 tablespoons soy sauce
2 teaspoons fresh parsley, chopped	2 tablespoons runny honey

Combine together the onion, garlic and grated ginger, plus the chopped parsley.

Add the liquid ingredients (lemon juice, sesame oil, soy sauce and honey).

Not only will this make an excellent marinade, but the mixture can also be brushed over meat when grilling or barbecuing.

A Marinade for Smoked Fish

Sometimes a marinade can be added to a dish in order subtly to change its taste rather than to tenderize the flesh. Many would say that any smoked fish has a delightful flavour all of its own and shouldn't be tampered with, but this particular recipe can also be used with other types of fish prior to being barbecued or grilled.

175ml/6fl oz olive oil
60ml/2fl oz lemon or lime juice
pinch of sugar

black pepper, freshly ground from a mill
2 teaspoons freshly chopped dill

Place the smoked fish fillets on to a large dinner plate.

Mix together the oil and juice (a screw-lidded jam jar is useful for this), add the sugar and a good couple of turns of pepper. Close the lid and shake vigorously before pouring over the fillets. Sprinkle over the dill.

Cover with cling-film and leave in the fridge to marinade for a couple of hours.

DIPS

Oh dear! Once again, we are heading towards possible confusion in giving 'dips' a separate subtitle – they might originally be derived from sweet chutneys, thickened sauces or relishes, but to most people nowadays the word conjures up small dishes of interestingly tasting 'pastes', into which one literally dips corn chips, tortillas or thin fingers of celery or carrots as a prelude to a main meal. This section assumes dips to be on that basis.

An attractive selection of easily made dips.

Horseradish and Watercress Cream

Although most dips work best by being eaten with tortilla chips or thin sticks of crispy vegetables, this one is perfect for dipping pieces of venison or beef sausages skewered on cocktail sticks. It is a firm favourite with the shooting guests on a West Sussex estate where it forms part of the mid-morning break.

5 tablespoons fresh watercress leaves, very finely chopped
4 tablespoons grated fresh horseradish (available in jars from supermarkets if you don't happen to grow your own)

200ml/7fl oz crème fraîche
½ tablespoon white wine vinegar
salt and ground black pepper, to season

In a bowl, stir together the chopped watercress, horseradish and crème fraîche. Add the wine vinegar; stir again and season well.

Salsa Verde

Most supermarkets offer a selection of dips in their chilled cabinet sections. Whilst most are good (and, of course, much depends on personal taste), there is a world of difference between the majority of salsas they provide and this truly Spanish (and extremely herby) authentic dish. Prepare at least two hours in advance of when it is required, but do not keep it overnight.

115g/4oz fresh parsley, *very* finely chopped
45g/1½oz either fresh chervil, chives, mint, or basil
30g/1oz red onion, peeled and finely chopped
30g/1oz capers, coarsely chopped

14g/½oz grated lime zest
125ml/4fl oz olive oil
salt and ground black pepper to taste

In a bowl, mix together all the ingredients, stir well and taste. Add more oil and salt if necessary (remembering that salt takes a little while to dissolve in cold dips).

Find a container into which the dip fits without leaving any air gaps and place into the refrigerator until required.

Pesto

Pesto is so useful – not least when added at the last minute to certain soups such as butternut squash. To make a dip, add it to mascarpone cheese.

30g/1oz fresh basil leaves
15g/½oz pine nuts
30g Parmesan cheese, freshly grated

1 garlic clove, peeled
5 tablespoons virgin olive oil
salt and ground black pepper to taste

Place all the ingredients in a blender, and mix into a paste.

Can there be anything more pleasurable than a summer glass of champagne and Guacamole dip taken by the poolside?

To make the dip, take a 250g/9oz pot of mascarpone and mix six tablespoons of pesto into it.

Guacamole

A section on dips cannot be considered complete without the inclusion of perhaps the most famous one of all. Not only can it be used as a dip, but it also makes a good starter when served on brown toast.

30g/1oz Spanish onion, peeled and finely
   chopped or grated
1 small green chilli, deseeded and finely chopped
4 sprigs fresh coriander leaves, finely chopped

¼ teaspoon salt
2 large avocados
1 large tomato, deseeded and chopped
30g/1oz red onion, finely chopped
1 tablespoon lime or lemon juice

Mix the Spanish onion, chilli, half the coriander and the salt in a mortar and pestle it into a paste.

Cut the avocados in half lengthways; remove the stone and spoon out the flesh into a mixing bowl before mashing it well and adding the pounded paste. Mix thoroughly, then stir in the tomato, red onion and remainder of the coriander.

Drizzle the lime/lemon juice over the surface; cover the bowl tightly with cling-film and place in the fridge until required.

Immediately before serving, stir and taste the guacamole and, if required, add a little seasoning.

NB: To make a hotter guacamole, leave the seeds in the green chilli but take great care when handling as they can react violently with your skin (and eyes), causing reddening and an extremely unpleasant 'burning' sensation. Alternatively, just add a dash or two of Tabasco.

Tzatziki Dip

Tzatziki is a traditional Greek appetizer and, like the recipe for Greek Relish, was kindly given to us by restaurateur Alexios Theophilus.

½ large cucumber, peeled and grated
sea salt (to weep, and to taste)
4 spring onions, peeled and finely sliced
500ml/18fl oz tub Greek yogurt

6 tablespoons fresh mint, finely chopped
1 garlic clove, peeled and crushed
juice of half a lemon

Place the cucumber in a colander and grind over a little sea salt. Leave it to stand for fifteen minutes in order for the salt to draw out the moisture from the cucumber.

Gently squeeze out any excess moisture before putting the cucumber into a mixing bowl and adding the remaining ingredients. Season to taste and keep in the fridge until required.

NB: This dip can be safely made and left for twenty-four hours. Add a little freshly ground black pepper just before serving.

Thousand Island Dip

Thousand Island salad dressing is well known. Adapt it a little; make it thicker and it becomes the perfect dip, as shown here.

150ml/5fl oz mayonnaise
150ml/5fl oz double cream
1 tablespoon lemon juice
¼ teaspoon paprika
2 tablespoons tomato ketchup (homemade, of course!)

4 gherkins, finely chopped
2 teaspoons horseradish sauce
2 teaspoons chives, finely chopped
1 garlic clove, peeled and crushed
salt and pepper to taste

In a large bowl, mix together all the ingredients. Cover with cling-film and refrigerate until required – no more than twenty-four hours.

AND FINALLY . . .

Tamarind Mustard

Several recipes in this book (especially those offered by Mary Hart) call for the inclusion of tamarind – a tree native to Africa and used in many Indian recipes for pickles and chutneys. It is the fruit of the tree that is most commonly used and, for cooking purposes, it is available in a variety of forms. On the assumption that you may have tamarind in the store cupboard as a result of trying some of the recipes that require its inclusion, we thought it would be of interest to describe a way of making tamarind mustard in order to create an unusual condiment. Okay, it's not technically a chutney, pickle, relish or ketchup, but perhaps we might be allowed to stretch a point?

115g/4oz tamarind block
150ml/5fl oz warm water
60g/2oz yellow mustard seeds

30g/1oz black mustard seeds
2 tablespoons honey (the clear variety)
a pinch each of ground cardamom and salt

Place the tamarind block into a mixing bowl and add the water. Leave it to soak for half an hour before taking a fork and breaking down the block until a paste is created. Push through a sieve and into a second bowl.

The mustard seeds should be ground in a small coffee grinder (or through a spice mill) and added to the tamarind together with all of the remaining ingredients.

Finally, spoon the tamarind mustard into sterilized jars, cover and seal. It can be stored for three to four months, but is ready to eat after three to four days.

Greek Traditional Grape Spoon-Sweet

The Greek 'Spoon-Sweet' is, as the name suggests, a sweet 'taster' traditionally served on a spoon and with coffee. Philip picked up this particular recipe whilst on holiday at the Medusa Resort Hotel, Naxos, Greece. It was given to him by Mariangela Karlovitch.

2kg/4lb 6oz grapes, washed and dried
1kg/2lb 3oz white sugar
200ml/7fl oz water

2 geranium leaves
juice of half a lemon
150g/5oz boiled non-salted almonds, peeled

Place the grapes in a hob-heatproof casserole and boil them with the sugar, the water, the geranium leaves and the lemon. Cook over a low heat for about half an hour.

Retain the mixture in the casserole overnight and the next day, boil them again for another twenty minutes, or until the grapes take a nice golden colour and the syrup thickens.

Add the almonds and store in a jar for up to a month.

Traditional Greek Spoon-Sweet (to the left of the photo can be seen an aubergine Spoon-Sweet – also well known in Greece).

Italian-Style Olives

Traditionally, olives are served with drinks, or as an appetizer along with other hors d'oeuvres. This recipe turns traditional into something far more interesting!

450g/1lb jar or tin of black olives in brine
rind of one orange, cut carefully into long, thin strips
rind of one large lemon, ditto

10 cloves garlic, carefully peeled and cut in half
1 tablespoon fresh thyme, chopped
olive oil, as much as is required to cover the ingredients in the preserving bottles

Drain as much brine as possible from the black olives and place them into a mixing bowl before adding all the other ingredients (excepting the olive oil). Stir together well.

Place the mixture into a preserving jar, completely covering the contents with olive oil and storing for at least a week before eating.

Blackberry or Raspberry Vinegar

According to *Farmhouse Kitchen II*, published by Trident Television in 1978 and from which this recipe is taken, this is an old-fashioned remedy for sore throats! It is, however, also 'good to eat with a plain steamed pudding' and is 'sometimes served in the North poured over hot Yorkshire pudding and eaten as a sweet course'.

450g/1lb fruit
600ml/1pt cider, or malt, vinegar (keep bottle for finished product)
450g/1lb granulated sugar (optional)

Put the fruit and vinegar into a glass or china bowl. Cover with a cloth and allow to stand for three to five days, stirring occasionally.

Strain off the liquid into a saucepan; set it over a low heat and add sugar, if used. Stir until dissolved. Boil the mixture for ten minutes, then pour it into the bottle.

NB: If you prefer not to add sugar during cooking, it may be added to taste when the vinegar is being used.

Crab Apple Jelly

A classic accompaniment to many dishes, Crab Apple Jelly is simple to make and requires little in the way of ingredients. Crab apples are small wild fruits that vary in colour from light green to yellow. The name 'crab' is thought to have originated from a Norse word meaning a small, rough tree. You can often come across crab apple trees in country hedgerows and the fruits occur in early autumn.

4kg/9lb crab apples
1kg/2lb 3oz caster sugar
juice of a lemon

Wash the apples and cut out the blossom heads and any bruised or insect-bitten sections. Place into a preserving pan and add sufficient water to cover all the apples. Bring to the boil before then simmering for twenty-five minutes or until the fruit is soft.

Pour the pulp into a straining bag or a similar arrangement made from several layers of muslin and let it drip overnight into a pan left underneath.

Next, measure the amount of juice given and combine with sugar at the proportion of ten parts of juice to seven parts of sugar. Add the lemon juice, then boil all the ingredients in order that the sugar might dissolve. Keep at a boiling roll for thirty-five to forty minutes, occasionally skimming off any froth that comes to the surface.

Test by removing a spoonful of the jelly and seeing if it sets once placed in the fridge. When it does, pour the remainder from the pan and into preserving jars. Seal whilst still warm (not hot) and store in a cool, dark place.

A straining bag is useful when making Crab Apple Jelly.

How to Use Chutneys and Pickles

Then, walking into the kitchen, Mrs Drydon, His Lordship's family cook, begged my tolerance for the 'un-holy mess in the place', giving as her reason that a pig had just been salted and put ready to hang and that the girls Florence and Mary had been 'at their wit's end, what with pickling and chutneying basketsful of stuff from the walled garden'. But what a glorious smell there was there: the almost nauseous stink of porcine flesh mixing with the sweetness of fruit and the dizziness of spices. The heat from the range was quite overpowering on a fine September day but it was a heady and glorious moment. Such thoughts were however quickly removed when Mrs Drydon, her earlier remorse for the state of her Empire seemingly forgotten, none too gently bustled me out saying that she was, 'busier than a yardful of chickens and no mistake'.

(John Forester, *A Little Country Knowledge*, 1879)

Smells undoubtedly affect the taste buds and the brain's perception of what the body is about to eat. A stale 'cabbage' smell – often as a result of experiences of schooldays and being forced to eat that which, as a youngster, one would prefer not to have done – can seriously have an effect on one's eating habits later in life, irrespective of the fact that freshly prepared cabbage can be a delight in so many ways.

Likewise, eyesight is equally important. In the case of Piccalilli, for example, so many people have been put off by the unnaturally vibrant, radioactive-looking yellowness of a commercially produced jar of the same, as a result of which they decline even to try it. Homemade chutneys, pickles, relishes, ketchups and dips are, however, a totally different thing altogether. Their colours are far more subtle and their vast variety of tastes make them appropriate for many an occasion.

The huge variety of homemade chutneys makes them appropriate for many an occasion – in this particular instance, Apple Cider Vinegar Chutney is served alongside a rabbit terrine.

WHAT GOES WITH WHAT

Although traditionally placed on the side of a plate as an attractive and tasty addition to a selection of cheeses, cold meats and salads, chutneys can be so much more than that. Try a sweet mango recipe for use in a toasted sandwich, or let one of the other sweet chutneys be the 'hero' of many a main course by serving it as a replacement for vegetables. Whilst it might seem obvious that they and pickles should be used as an accompaniment to cold meats, Ploughman's Lunches and at any occasion where cheese is involved, both can be used more subtly in order to enhance the most unlikely of dishes.

Because we needed to photograph both it and the cooking process for this book, Jeremy made a huge batch of Runner Bean Chutney. Afterwards, bottled and 'ready to go', several jars sat in the fridge for a couple of days until guests began to arrive (at which point perhaps we should tell you that almost every day in August, Jeremy and his wife have visitors to their home in France; some staying for a time and some, being simply French neighbours, just here in the house for an evening meal). Perhaps due to its sweetness, that particular recipe was a huge hit and it was used to accompany English breakfasts of bacon and egg, as a spread for croissants, with cheese at lunchtime, evening barbeques, appropriate puddings and as a base for some unique dips suitable for preprandial dunking (we say 'unique' purely because of the fact that the best dips are often created by simply adding minor ingredients, which happen to be on hand, to an existing element). At the last scrapings, the remainder of this particular batch of chutney was then added to casseroles

Chutney can be added to casseroles and curries in order to impart a subtle additional taste and sweetness.

and curries, where it provided a subtle texture and sweetness – a logical move from the fact that I learned many years ago whereby just a spoonful of jam or marmalade will add 'zest' and interest to a potentially boring stew, jus or gravy.

Chutneys

Most chutneys go with almost anything, but, as a general guide, try fiery ones with sausages and merely spicy ones with turkey, coleslaw and jacket potatoes. When you are considering serving chutney alongside a salad dish accompanied by a little cold meat or fish, a really peppery leaf from watercress, or what is considered by many to be the perfectly delightful taste of wild rocket will enhance the flavour of both the main part of the meal and the chutney. Some, such as the Rapid Rhubarb Chutney, go very well with fish such as smoked mackerel or grilled freshly caught trout and can either be made and stored, or made at the time and spooned over the fish whilst still warm. Red Onion Marmalade (which is basically chutney) will go well with not only hunks of cheese and fresh bread for lunch, but is also superb when accompanying a goat's cheese tartlet as a starter.

Pickles

In India, no matter whether it be the simplest fare of rice, vegetables and yogurt, or a hugely complex preparation involving over a hundred ingredients, a meal is often considered incomplete without a spoonful of pickle to liven it up. Sometimes, rather

Tomato Chutney and cheese.

than playing a supporting role, they become the star of the show and absolutely vital to the character of the dish. By contrast, hardly any pub Ploughman's Lunch in the UK comes to the table without the inclusion of a few pickled onions. For the most part, they are bland commercially produced affairs and their almost watery vinegar does nothing more than seep across the plate and soaks the bottom of a lump of cheese or piece of cold meat. However, replace them with the crunchy robust onions made at home and you have a different meal altogether. In most fish and chip shops, there are jars of both pickled onions and pickled eggs on the back shelves. Use those you've made yourself to accompany traditional fish and chips and again you will taste a remarkable difference.

The juices from pickled produce does not have to be thrown away once the jar's contents have been eaten. It has a multitude of further uses ranging from marinating meat, adding to sauces, dips and soups, and as a dressing over salads (be cautious with how much you add to the latter – a little pickling juice goes a long way).

Relishes and Beyond
Relishes can obviously be used in sandwiches, on salads, as side condiments, or wrapped in meats. Be imaginative; if you suddenly realize that an instant relish is in order, follow the four 'C' method – Choose what ingredients you have, then Chop, Cook and Create. Provided that you follow the basic cooking patterns featured in the previous chapter, very rarely will it be a failure. Make interesting picnic parcels by not only including freshly

Pickled onions – love 'em or hate 'em!

made relishes as an accompaniment, but also by wrapping them in cold slices of ham, or thinly cut roast beef (Horseradish Sauce is traditional – but why not try Beetroot and Cabbage Relish, see Chapter 5).

Ketchups should be used as they were originally intended when developed in the Far East and work well in complementing some types of seafood. Try what you make spooned over pasta dishes. Nor do all ketchups need to be eaten either – commercial tomato ketchup is known to be good for helping to buff up copper pans and even as a hair conditioner! Apart from a brief mention in the Introduction and a subsequent single recipe in Chapter 5, nothing much has been made of coleslaw. It is, nevertheless, an exciting and imaginative addition to any last-minute picnic and also works well with barbecued foods such as chicken pieces and French fries. If you don't like cabbage, use broccoli and make Broccolislaw, or Caulislaw in a Dreamy, Creamy Dressing (see Chapter 5). Purists might think them just beyond the scope of this book, but to us they are worth including in order to encourage the reader's imagination.

SHOWING

Showing your chutneys and pickles is not, as it used to be, simply the preserve (forgive the pun!) of older village matriarchs at the local flower show. Over recent years, the

Baguette, Brie and Plum Relish.

numbers of entries at small village events and at those much larger affairs held nationally have been ever-increasing. Whether this has been caused by a greater interest in showing by longstanding chutney and pickle making enthusiasts, or just a greater interest in chutney and pickle making in general is open to conjecture. No matter what the reason, there is, however, a considerable skill in producing something that the judges will like and indicate their approval by awarding it First Prize.

It is not simply enough to create something good enough to eat – although you should, of course, always taste-test the batch of chutneys or pickles that you intend to exhibit – consistency and colour are just as important. Jars and bottles, although they can be any shape, ought not to be too large, arguably around 225g/8oz size; be of clear glass; and show no commercial markings of any description. They should be clean, polished (with a vinegar solution for best results) and have no telltale fingermarks (always make a point of giving your entry a final wipe over as you set it in place on the exhibition bench). All jars and bottles must have a suitably attractive and airtight lid and it is worth remembering that there is very little point in attempting to exhibit anything that is less than at least three months old, as the flavours will not have had time to mature. There is an accepted rule of thumb whereby jams made in the summer can be shown in the autumn of the current year, but chutneys and pickles should not make their appearance on the exhibition bench until the following autumn.

Renowned marmalade and chutney maker Mary Hart with one of her many trophies.

Show Schedules

It is important that you read the show schedule carefully and write up the necessary jar and/or bottle labels as per the schedule. The label should tell the reader precisely what is in the jar or bottle and also the date when it was made. It must not contain your name and address. Having checked on the closing date for entries, you will need to submit a completed entry form in order to have each individual exhibit recorded by either the show secretary or their steward. In return, you will be allocated a numbered ticket, which is generally left with your exhibit on the show bench and is your only identification until after judging takes place. If you are one of the lucky ones, your name will then appear on a coloured card denoting First, Second, Third, or maybe Highly Commended. Win or lose, judges will often write constructive comments on your ticket, which should hopefully prove useful to you in the future. But even the most tyrannical of judges cannot be as fearsome as the prospect, which even today faces new brides in some parts of India, where they are expected to show their cooking skills to their in-laws by presenting them with a selection of pickles!

Whether in India or not, there is a fine art to preparing and showing chutneys and pickles, and it will undoubtedly be in your interest to find someone knowledgeable in your locality who can give you guidance regarding how best to go about it. Be warned though: exhibiting chutneys, pickles and relishes can be very addictive. Suddenly you'll find yourself eyeing up crab apples, for instance, not with a view to producing a tasty pickle to set amongst the Boxing Day table of cold meats, but more towards the date of a particular show or exhibition and that elusive cup for 'Best in Show'.

MARKET FORCES

Putting aside the pleasure to be gained from exhibiting the produce from your kitchen and the delight on the faces of your friends and family when presented with either a spoonful at a mealtime, or a jar as a gift, there can be no doubt that homemade and traditional chutneys, pickles and relishes are enjoying something of a resurgence. Whether it is a general trend brought about as a result of financial issues, whereby many are making an effort to save money where they can, an increased awareness of how many air miles particular products have to travel before reaching the supermarket shelf, or the 'feel-good' factor of self-sufficiency, we have no real idea, but the fact remains that making creative chutneys, pickles and relishes is on the increase. This is perhaps rather strange when one considers the fact that, commercially, the sales of mass-produced products appear to be on the decrease.

Market research by Mintel (international advisors to the Great and the Good) has it that whilst chutneys have been a long-time staple meal accompaniment for the older generation of shoppers, youngsters are not, beyond a lunchtime cheese and pickle sandwich, buying with the same eagerness. This is somewhat incomprehensible when bearing in mind the fact that as a result of eating out, they are being exposed to a far greater variety of tastes, for example when dipping their poppadums into a bowl of Mango Chutney – an experience one might suppose they would like to replicate when eating an Indian-type meal at home. Mintel also suggests that current food trends have made everyone focus on eating fresh, rather than pickled fruit and vegetables, as a result of which, sales have stalled and there is very little expectation of a market growth for at least another three years. Apparently a drop in overall bread consumption has also had a detrimental effect on chutneys and pickles being used as a sandwich filling.

Perhaps it's not so strange? Perhaps the proof of the pudding is in the eating and the reason supermarket sales of chutneys, pickles and relishes are dropping is simply due to the likes of you, the many contributors and the authors of this book who are all part of an ever-growing band of enthusiasts willing to settle for nothing but the best; the best being that which is lovingly created at home from fresh and exciting produce. Pass over a hunk of freshly baked bread, a chunk of Judy Bell's Wensleydale Cheese, a spoonful of home-made Runner Bean Chutney and that will do for lunch. We could have salmon, wild rocket and Rapid Rhubarb Chutney . . . or perhaps roast beef with a little Cauliflower Pickle . . . there again, something with Field Mushroom Relish sounds rather appealing.

Choice and opportunity is always the answer, as can be evidenced by the remarks of J. E. Marriat-Ferguson, in his book *Visiting Home*, published in 1905. They make a fitting conclusion to this particular book.

> In Africa I'd lived in a confused world. I was there to do a job
> of work but there were many times of inactivity. The annex
> between Zululand and Natal was completed a long while ago.
> What will happen with Chief Bambatha, is open to question; I
> think there might be an uprising – and very shortly at that.
> What a change to have decent food at the club, and with

friends, now I'm in London. In Africa, I seemed only to be offered guinea-fowl as meat. As for improving the taste I gave thanks for Dutty chutney – such fowl would otherwise be a desperately dry meat cooked as it is. The biscuits imported from the Liverpool warehouse of W & R Jacob were tolerable, especially when topped with Jalapenos pickle. Last evening at the club, René recommended the roast beef. Thankfully it came with the chef's own horseradish sauce: I knew I was home; even if only visiting . . .

Plum, Pear and Carrot Pickle – the nearest thing to Branston!

Glossary

achar Hindi term for pickle.

al dente Italian term used to describe the texture of slight resistance when bitten.

allspice dried berry of the pimento tree of the clove family.

aniseed seeds used to flavour pickles, chutneys and curries.

arrowroot sometimes used as a substitute for cornflour as a thickening agent; unlike cornflour, it produces a clear sauce. Might be used in making relishes.

asafoetida hard, resinous gum, used in the preparation of pickle masala. It is sold in blocks or pieces as a gum and more frequently as a fine yellow powder, sometimes crystalline or granulated.

bain-marie shallow-sided container, which is half-filled with boiling water and sometimes used to help seal freshly bottled ketchups.

beurre manié a sauce or relish thickener of softened butter combined with an equal amount of flour.

black pepper black pepper is the immature berries (white pepper is the mature berries with the hull removed). Use whole when pickling, ground on most other occasions.

blanch a cooking technique of placing food into boiling water for a short time, then in cold water to stop cooking.

bouquet garni herbs tied or bagged in muslin and used to flavour soups or casseroles.

brining immersing raw vegetables in a strong salt and water solution prior to pickling.

brown soft sugar looks as its name suggests and is used in pickles and chutneys.

cardamom seed seeds belonging to the ginger family.

cayenne true cayenne pepper is very hot and should be used only in small quantities (pinches or less). This pepper is usually red or yellow and long and slender. It can be purchased whole, but it is commonly found as dried and ground.

celeriac the root of a variety of celery, used raw or cooked in a variety of chutneys and pickles.

celery salt or seed pungent seed from the celery plant. Used in coleslaws, relishes and pickles.

chervil a mild, aniseed-flavoured herb related to parsley.

chilli peppers many varieties from mild to hot.

concasser to chop roughly or pound in a mortar.

coriander seed   standard ingredient in most Indian dishes and pickles; coriander seeds are used whole or in coarse or fine powder form. This herb is of the carrot family and has the flavour of sage and lemon peel. When stocking your pantry get both the seeds and the powder.

demerara sugar   darker in colour than golden caster sugar but still free-flowing.

dice   to cut food into small cubes of about 5mm (¼ in) across.

dill seed   dried fruit of the dill plant and perfect for pickles.

dill weed   aromatic herb pertaining to the carrot family and used in similar situations to dill seed.

dry-roast   some recipes call for seeds to be 'dry-roasted'. The easiest way to do this is to place them in a frying pan to which no oil has been added. The natural oils from the seeds or nuts are sufficient to 'roast' them, but they need tossing, or kept on the move with a wooden spatula so as not to burn them. The process will take no more than a couple of minutes.

emonder   to skin tomatoes etc., by plunging them into boiling water for a few seconds and then dipping them into cold water.

fennel seeds   used in much the same way as aniseed seeds.

fenugreek   an ancient herb; fenugreek is the seeds from a bean-like plant.

fines herbes   a mixture of finely chopped herbs, traditionally chervil, chives, parsley and tarragon.

garam masala   adds flavour and fragrance to Indian dishes, including chutneys and pickles. It is a combination of various whole spices. You can buy it ready made in the stores or make your own.

ginger   pungent root of a plant grown in China, Japan, India and the West Indies. Useful in many pickles, chutney and preserves.

gremolata   very finely chopped lemon zest, juice and parsley.

hermetic seal   an absolutely airtight container seal, which prevents re-entry of air or micro-organisms into packaged foods.

hulling   removing the stalk and leaves from soft fruits such as strawberries.

infuse   to brew in hot water or other liquids to extract flavour.

julienne   sliced vegetables cut into matchstick-sized pieces, either by the use of a knife or mandolin.

Kilner jar   glass jar which has a lid in two sections to create an airtight seal. Originally a glass disc sat on top of the jar and secured in place with a metal screw band which contained a rubber seal. The original Kilner jar is often confused with the more widely available glass jars with a rubber seal and a metal hinge, which when closed forms an airtight seal. The latter type are nowadays more often used in creative chutney and pickle making, but erroneously given the generic name of 'Kilner jars'.

legumes   any member of the pea family, including chick peas, runner beans, soya beans and lentils.

Le Parfait jars   preserving jars similar to Kilner jars, but originating in France.

mace   Covering of the inner shell that holds nutmeg; use whole in pickling.

mandolin   not in this instance, a musical instrument, but a slicer used to produce julienne vegetables.

marinade a liquid and/or herb mix in which meat and game is left for several hours. See *also* 'marinate'.

marinate to add liquid or dry ingredients (or a mixture of the two, such as wine and herbs) to meat or fish in order to impart flavour or tenderize.

mirepoix coarsely diced vegetables

mixed spice classically, a mixture containing caraway, allspice, coriander, cumin, nutmeg and ginger. Particularly useful when pickling.

oxidation chemical process in which a substance combines with oxygen; for example, when an apple turns brown after it has been peeled or cut open.

parboil to partially cook food by boiling briefly in water.

peppercorns most often used whole. If required in powdered form, they taste best when freshly ground.

pickling straight forwardly, the practice of adding enough vinegar or lemon juice to a low-acid food to reduce its pH to 4.6 or lower.

pinch an approximate measure of any ingredient, but usually an amount held between thumb and forefinger.

pudhina Indian name for mint leaves. Mint is used in vegetable dishes, as a garnish and in chutneys.

reduce to reduce a liquid-based mixture by boiling until it thickens to the right consistency.

refresh most commonly used in reference to blanched vegetables that are placed immediately in ice water to stop the cooking, set the colour and restore the crispness. Greens and herbs that are still very fresh, but have gone limp, can be restored to their original state by placing in cold water and then patted dry.

sachet a small pouch, similar to a teabag, filled with dried herbs.

spice bag homemade muslin bag used to hold spices in order that they might add flavour to a pickling solution without leaving a bitter, unpleasant aftertaste.

stabilizers substances that help to stabilize the structure of food and help to prevent any unwanted chemical changes as well as help it thicken. Gelatin and pectin are examples of commonly used stabilizers.

strew to draw out moisture from watery vegetables such as marrows and courgettes by sprinkling them with salt and leaving them overnight.

suer see 'sweat'

sweat cooking foods, such as onions, over medium heat until they soften without burning and browning.

tamarind a fruit, available dried or as a paste. Can sometimes be used in place of or replaced by, lime juice.

tindora vegetable: type of gherkin, which may be eaten green and immature, or red and mature. Used in some Indian-based pickles.

translucent cooking (onions, for example) until clear or transparent.

turmeric mustard-flavoured root, plant of the ginger family.

vacuum technically, the state of negative pressure and reflects how thoroughly air is removed from within a jar of processed food – the higher the vacuum, the less air left in the jar.

weeping *see* 'strew'

white sugar refined brown sugar, useful when it's important that pickle and chutney colours are retained.

zest the coloured rind of citrus fruit, normally grated or cut into thin slivers and used as additional flavouring. Zest contains vital oils, but to avoid a bitterness of taste, grate or pare the rind thinly, avoiding the pith.

Chutneys, pickles, relishes and ketchups bring life to any meal – be it a simple lunch or an exotic dinner party.

At a Glance Recipe List

This helps you by identifying the main ingredients. Although alphabetically ordered here, it will, however, be necessary to refer to the Index for the page on which a particular recipe appears. Some, such as the Uncooked Green Tomato Chutney, for example, have equal quantities of ingredients – in this case tomatoes and apples, and it so appears under both the apple section below and that appertaining to tomatoes. Other, more 'minor', ingredients feature only in the Index.

APPLES

Apple and Pear Chutney
Apple and Tomato Chutney
Apple Chutney – Mild and
　　Fruity
Apple Chutney – Really
　　Spicy
Apple Ketchup
Apple, Onion and Mint Pickle
Clod Hall Chutney
Crab Apple Chutney
Crab Apple Jelly
Fat Olive's Chutney
Kent Windfall Chutney
Marrow and Apple Chutney
Stephan Langton Chutney
Uncooked Green Tomato
　　Chutney

APRICOTS

Apricot Chutney

ASPARAGUS

Asparagus in Pickled Onion
　　Juice

BANANAS

Banana, Date and Mango
　　Chutney
Caribbean Chutney

BEETROOT

Beetroot and Cabbage
　　Relish
Beetroot Relish
Sweet Beetroot Chutney

BLACKBERRIES

Blackberry or Raspberry
　　Vinegar
Walton Heath Blackberry
　　Chutney

BROCCOLI

Broccolislaw

BUTTERNUT SQUASH

Butternut, Apricot and
　　Almond Chutney

CABBAGE

Beetroot and Cabbage
　　Relish
Cabbage Coleslaw
Red Cabbage and Apple
　　Chutney
Red Cabbage Pickle

CARROTS

Carrot and Almond Relish
Carrot Chutney

CAULIFLOWER

Cauliflower Pickle
Caulislaw with Dreamy,
    Creamy Dressing
Chow-Chow
Military Pickle
Piccalilli

CELERY

Chow-Chow
Chris and Felicity's Celery
    and Fennel Relish

COURGETTES

Chow-Chow
Fiery Marrow and Cour-
    gette Chutney
Red Onion and Courgette
    Chutney
Spicy Ratatouille Chutney

CRANBERRIES

Cranberry, Orange and
    Vodka Relish
Quick Cranberry Relish

CUCUMBERS

Chow-Chow
Pickled Cucumbers
Pickled Gherkins
Tzatziki Dip

DAMSONS

Damson Sauce

EGGS

Pickled Eggs

ELDERBERRIES

Elderberry Ketchup
Elderberry Pickle

FENNEL

Chris and Felicity's Celery
    and Fennel Relish
Theo's Pickled Fennel

FIGS

Australian Fig, Thyme and
    Raisin Chutney

GOOSEBERRIES

Gooseberry Chutney
Gooseberry, Orange and
    Pistachio Relish

GRAPES

Greek Traditional Grape
    Spoon-Sweet

HORSERADISH

Horseradish and Water-
    cress Cream

LAVENDER

Beatrice Laval's Lavender
    Chutney

LIMES

Indian Lime Pickle
Pickling limes

MAGNOLIA FLOWERS

Pickled Magnolia Flowers

MANGOES

Microwave Mango Pickle

MARROWS

Fiery Marrow and Cour-
    gette Chutney
Marrow and Apple
    Chutney
Marrow Pickle
Military Pickle

MELONS

Mildly Spicy Melon Pickle

MUSHROOMS

Field Mushroom Relish
Mushroom Ketchup
Pickled Christmas Field
    Mushrooms in Olive Oil

NUTS

Carrot and Almond Relish
Gooseberry, Orange and
    Pistachio Relish
Greek Traditional Grape
    Spoon-Sweet (almonds)
Pesto (pine nuts)
Pistachio and Sesame Seed
    Cream
Walnut and Coriander
    Relish
Walnut Ketchup

OLIVES

Italian-Style Olives

ONIONS

Apple, Onion and Mint
  Pickle
Chow-Chow
Ginger and Garlic
  Marinade
Onion Marmalade Chutney
Onion Relish
Red Onion and Courgette
  Chutney
Red Onion Marmalade
Rhubarb and Orange
  Chutney

ORANGES

Cranberry, Orange and
  Vodka Relish
Gooseberry, Orange and
  Pistachio Relish
Goosnargh Orange and
  Lemon Chutney
Rhubarb and Orange
  Chutney

PARSLEY

Salsa Verde

PEACHES

Golden Glory Peach Pickle

PEARS

Apple and Pear Chutney
Pear and Raisin Chutney
Fat Olive's Chutney
Fresh Pear Chutney

Kent Windfall Chutney
Pickled Spice Pears
West Country Pear
  Chutney

PEPPERS

Caribbean Chutney
Chilli Jam Relish
Pepper Pot Pickle
Pickled Peppers
Sweet Pepper Relish

PINEAPPLE

Pineapple Chilli Pickle
Spiced Pineapple Pickle

PLUMS

Damson Sauce
Plum, Pear and Carrot
  Pickle
Worcester Plum Pickle

RHUBARB

Rapid Rhubarb Chutney
Rhubarb and Orange
  Chutney
Rhubarb Relish
Wakefield Rhubarb
  Chutney

RUNNER BEANS

Chow-Chow
Military Pickle
Runner Bean Chutney

SAMPHIRE

Marsh Samphire Pickle

SHALLOTS

Chow-Chow
Pickled Shallots
Shallots in Balsamic Vinegar

TAMARIND

Tamarind Mustard

TINDORA

Tindora Pickle

TOMATOES

Apple and Tomato Chutney
Blackfriars Tomato
  Ketchup
Chilli Jam Relish
Chow-Chow
Easy Balsamic and Tomato
  Relish
Onion and Cherry Tomato
  Chutney
Red Tomato Chutney
Spiced Tomato Chutney
Spicy Ratatouille Chutney
Uncooked Green Tomato
  Chutney

WALNUTS

Walnut and Coriander
  Relish
Walnut Ketchup

WATERCRESS

Horseradish and Water-
  cress Cream

Index

The names of recipes are shown in *italics*

air miles 6
Apple and Pear Chutney 46
Apple and Tomato Chutney 56
Apple Chutney – Mild and Fruity 51–52
Apple Chutney – Really Spicy 49–50
Apple Ketchup 112–113
Apple, Onion and Mint Pickle 44, 78
Apricot Chutney 69
Asparagus in Pickled Onion Juice 87–88
asparagus 88
Australian Fig, Thyme and Raisin Chutney 52–53

bacteria 19, 20, 24
baking soda 19
Banana, Date and Mango Chutney 52
Beatrice Laval's Lavender Chutney 67
Beetroot 33, 36
Beetroot and Cabbage Relish 101
Beetroot Relish 100–101
Blackberry Vinegar 124
Blackfriars Tomato Ketchup 115
bottles, filling of 21–22
brining 28
Broccolislaw 109–110
Brodie, Lynn 4, 23, 25, 48, 53
Butternut, Apricot and Almond Chutney 54

Cabbage Coleslaw 109
Caribbean Chutney 48, 53–54
Carrot and Almond Relish 101
Carrot Chutney 62
carrots, growing of 37

cauliflower 25, 37
Cauliflower Pickle 85–86
Cauliflower with Dreamy, Creamy Dressing 110
Chilli Jam Relish 99–100
Chow-Chow 83–84
Chris and Felicity's Celery and Fennel Relish 105–106
chutneys 40–73
    as gifts 7, 17, 18
    history of 9
    testing for 'setting' 40
'chutnification' 10
cider vinegar 26
Cleopatra 8, 98
Clod Hall Chutney 54–56
courgettes 36
Coleslaw 10
Crab Apple Chutney 52
Crab Apple Jelly 124–125
Cranberry, Orange and Vodka Relish 105

Damson Sauce 115–116
dips 118
dried fruits 34

Easy Balsamic and Tomato Relish 104
Eggs 38–39
Elderberry Ketchup 113
Elderberry Pickle 77–78

Fat Olives' Chutney 45
Field Mushroom Relish 109

Fiery Marrow and Courgette Chutney 64–65
Fresh Pear Chutney 41
fruits 32, 34
    dried 34
    making the best of 25, 32–34
funnels 15

garlic 36
Ginger and Garlic Marinade 117
Golden Glory Peach Pickle 81–82
Gooseberry Chutney 42
Gooseberry, Orange and Pistachio Relish 103
Goosnargh Orange and Lemon Chutney 46–47
Greek Relish 108
Greek Traditional Grape Spoon-Sweet 123
green tomato chutney 30, 36, 67–68
Guacamole 121

Hall & Woodhouse, brewers 42, 81–82
Hart, Mary 4, 14, 22, 30, 40, 46, 49–50, 54, 56, 57, 58, 62, 63, 66, 75, 79, 122
herbs 38
Horseradish and Watercress Cream 119
Horseradish relish 11
hygiene 19–22

Indian Lime Pickle 82–83
ingredients, sourcing 32–34
Italian Style Olives 124

jars 15
    filling of 21–22, 40
    sizes 16–17, 40
    sterilizing 15, 21–22, 36
    types used for storage 15–17

Kent Windfall Chutney 47–48
ketchups 112–115
Kilner jars 16, 17

ladles 14–15
Lakeland Ltd 12, 17, 19

legalities, appertaining to selling 7–8
lemons 32
lids for jars 17–18, 23
limes 31

marinades 116–118
    Ginger and Garlic 117
Marrow and Apple Chutney 66
Marrow Pickle 84–85
Marsh Samphire Pickle 90
microwave 21
Microwave Mango Pickle 80
Mildly Spicy Melon Pickle 76–77
Military Pickle 81
Mushroom Ketchup 112
mushrooms, collecting of 33–34, 87
mustard pickle see 'Piccalilli'

National Farmer's Retail and Markets Association (FARMA) 8

oils 24, 30–31
Onion and Cherry Tomato Chutney 56–57
Onion Marmalade Chutney 67
Onion Relish 103
onions; growing of 35
Oyster Ketchup 10

Pepper Pot Pickle 74–75
pestle (and mortar) 29
Pesto 119–120
Piccalilli 25, 37, 88, 89
Pickled Cucumbers 94–95
Pickled Eggs 38–39, 96–97
Pickled Field Christmas Mushrooms in Olive Oil 87
Pickled Gherkins 96
pickled herrings 10
Pickled Magnolia Flowers 90–91
Pickled Peppers 96
Pickled Shallots 93
Pickled Spice Pears 91, 115
pickles 74–98
pickling 85

pickling lime 31
Pineapple Chilli Pickle 75–76
Pistachio and Sesame Seed Cream 110–111
ploughman's lunch 9, 42
Plum, Pear and Carrot Pickle 79–80
'Pontac' Ketchup 10, 113

Quick Cranberry Relish 106

Rapid Rhubarb Chutney 44–45
Red Cabbage and Apple Chutney 64
Red Cabbage Pickle 86–87
Red Onion and Courgette Chutney 69–71
Red Tomato Chutney 57–58
relishes 9–10, 99–109
Rhubarb and Orange Chutney 44
Rhubarb Relish 106–108
Runner Bean Chutney 59–62

salsa 10, 99
Salsa Verdé 119
salt 25, 28
shallots, growing of 35
    pickling of 93
Shallots in Balsamic Vinegar 93–94
sieves 15
Slater, Nigel 57
Spiced Pineapple Pickle 75
Spiced Tomato Chutney 58
spices 29–30
Spicy Ratatouille Chutney 62–63
spoons 14–15

Stephan Langton Chutney 71–73
sterilizing 20, 21, 22
Stobart, Tom 4, 10, 28, 116
storage 18, 22–24
sugar 28
Sweet Beetroot Chutney 63–64
Sweet Pepper Relish 103–104

Tamarind Mustard 122
Theo's Pickled Fennel 89
Thousand Island Dip 122
Tindora Pickle 83
Tomato Ketchup 83
tomatoes, growing of 36
Tsatziki Dip 121–122

Uncooked Green Tomato Chutney 67–68
utensils 12–18

vegetables 35–37
    making the best of 25, 32–34
vinegar 24, 26–27, 39

Wakefield Rhubarb Chutney 45
Walnut and Coriander Relish 108
Walnut Ketchup 114
Walters, Jonathan 25, 28
Walton Heath Blackberry Chutney 48–49
wartime measure 6
West Country Pear Chutney 42
Worcester Plum Pickle 80–81